STEPS IN WRITING THE RESEARCH PAPER

ROBERTA H. MARKMAN, Ph.D., Professor
CALIFORNIA STATE UNIVERSITY,
LONG BEACH, CALIFORNIA

PETER T. MARKMAN, Professor
FULLERTON COLLEGE,
FULLERTON, CALIFORNIA

AND

MARIE L. WADDELL, Former Professor
THE UNIVERSITY OF TEXAS
EL PASO, TEXAS

Third Edition

BARRON'S EDUCATIONAL SERIES, INC.
WOODBURY, NEW YORK • LONDON • TORONTO • SYDNEY

© Copyright, 1982 by Barron's Educational Series, Inc.

Prior editions © Copyright, 1971, 1965 by Barron's Educational Series, Inc.

All inquiries should be addressed to
Barron's Educational Series, Inc.
113 Crossways Park Drive
Woodbury, New York 11797

Library of Congress Catalog Card No. 81-22891

International Standard Book No. 0-8120-2023-5

Library of Congress Cataloging in Publication Data

Markman, Roberta H.
  10 steps in writing the research paper.

  Includes index.
  1. Report writing.   I. Markman, Peter T.   II. Waddell, Marie L.
III. Title.   IV. Title: Ten steps in writing the research paper.
PE1478.M3   1982   001.4   81-22891
ISBN 0-8120-2023-5   AACR2

PRINTED IN THE UNITED STATES OF AMERICA

5   800   9

CONTENTS

PREFACE TO THE THIRD EDITION

We are delighted that the success of this manual in meeting the needs of both the high school student and the graduate scholar now, on the twentieth anniversary of its first printing, warrants a third edition. Experienced research writers have profited from the manual's suggested techniques and the numerous models for correct form; inexperienced students have felt the security of being able to follow definite steps in order to write papers with the least wasted effort, the greatest accuracy in form, and the assurance that the finished papers would meet the most exacting standards of scholarly research. The methodology outlined herein, the succinctness of its presentation, and the extensive coverage of its forms have received praise from both students and instructors throughout the country during the past twenty years.

Although this new edition retains the compact format for which the earlier two have been praised, all the materials have been updated to include various changes in forms for documentation, new sources for basic reference, and a new documented paper with a profusion of accompanying footnotes and an extensive bibliography to illustrate every conceivable form and technique for the student. In addition, the outline for the new paper is written to exemplify a comparative study with an interdisciplinary approach; it represents a new and important focus in education and a challenging area for further research. The sample paper itself is designed to develop only the thesis for the outline, but no problem of documentation is ignored.

We have each had the marvelous experience of sending our students off with this manual as their only "instructor" and of receiving creative and accurately documented research in return. We therefore feel confident that this third edition will do an even better job of instructing and of making the process of writing the research paper a process of ten easy steps.

HUNTINGTON HARBOUR, CALIFORNIA
JANUARY 1, 1982

Roberta Hoffman Markman
Peter Tollin Markman

INTRODUCTION TO RESEARCH

Research is the disciplined process of investigating and seeking facts which will lead one to discover the truth about something. This truth, stated as one's thesis,* must come as a result of the facts one discovers, and it must be proved conclusively by the facts selected. The thesis may not be a statement of preconceived opinion or prejudice; the research paper may not be a stringing together of related quotations and a collection of footnotes.

The research paper, a formal presentation of these discovered facts, provides the evidence one needs to defend the opinion expressed as the thesis. Consequently, one must state how and where these facts were found. If they were discovered from what other people have said or written, the student must tell who said them and where they were said so that the reader could find them also; if they were discovered by direct observation, the student must describe this experience so that the reader could repeat it and observe the same phenomena or facts. The opinion, which is the thesis, is subjectively presented; the facts, which provide the supporting points, are objectively presented.

During the process of research, the student learns to select, evaluate, and analyze facts; to discipline habits of thought and work; and, most important, to think—to create a new angle of vision. In this sense only, the research paper is original; but it is important enough in itself to justify the work involved in its creation.

Because nothing else so clearly reveals the true quality and merit of the writer's mind, the research paper becomes a valid criterion for judging the disciplined work habits and the intellectual maturity of the student.

*See Research Terms Defined, pp. 112–115.

1

THE TEN STEPS IN RESEARCH

There is always more than one way of accomplishing any task, and doing research is no exception. After much trial and error, the experienced researcher usually arrives at some system which has proved itself to be the best for him or her. However the individual systems may vary, there are ten basic steps that provide a logical method for research and result in an ease of procedure for the researcher, the ultimate economy of time and effort, the assurance that comes from following a time-tested procedure, accuracy in the result, and the most universal acceptance by examining scholars. As you proceed, you may think that you can eliminate a step or two in the process, only to find later that you have created some extra ones to make up for the detour. So watch your step!

Step	1	FIND A SUBJECT.
Step	2	READ A GENERAL ARTICLE OR TWO.
Step	3	FORMULATE A TEMPORARY THESIS AND A TEMPORARY OUTLINE.
Step	4	PREPARE THE BIBLIOGRAPHY.
Step	5	TAKE NOTES FROM RELEVANT SOURCES.
Step	6	LABEL NOTECARDS; REVISE THE WORKING OUTLINE.
Step	7	WRITE THE FIRST DRAFT.
Step	8	REVISE THE TEXT; WRITE AN INTRODUCTION AND A CONCLUSION.
Step	9	FILL IN FOOTNOTES ON THE DRAFT.
Step	10	PUT THE PAPER IN ITS FINAL FORM.

STEP

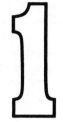

FIND A SUBJECT

Finding a topic that will interest you, one that is worth your time to investigate and one for which you will have the necessary time and materials, is an extremely important step in writing the research paper. You need not be familiar with a subject before doing research on it, but you should have some interest in the general area it involves because you will be working with that subject for a long period of time.

When the general subject is not assigned by your instructor, you can usually find one by examining your own interests, your background, or the other courses you are studying. There are other considerations that will limit the possibilities from which you may choose.

Your choice of a suitable subject for investigation will often be determined by whether or not you are interested in reading or investigating—and consequently analyzing—the original material directly and therefore working with primary sources* or whether you are interested in investigating what others have said about your subject and therefore working with secondary sources. The usual college assignment involves the latter. Your choice will be determined further when you eliminate unsuitable subjects. Some subjects are not worth investigating; they are either too trivial, merely factual, or obviously routine. Others are often too new or

---

*See Research Terms Defined, pp. 112–115.

current for conclusive study; a research paper must be factual, not conjectural, and must therefore be based on a variety of sources. The availability of resource materials will vary with time and locale, so you must know your area and your library. And finally, some subjects have never been suitable for research: a biography summarized from secondary sources, the entire history of anything, or any subject that you will investigate with a closed mind.

STEP

READ A GENERAL ARTICLE

After you have decided on a subject, the next step is to read a general, authoritative article (such as one in the *Encyclopaedia Britannica* or *Americana*) so that you can see what the possibilities and ramifications of the subject are. You will, in this first investigation, find out whether a subject is too broad to use without strict limitation or too narrow to consider at all. You will also orient yourself and become familiar with the general area in which you will be working. This reading will not only suggest ideas about how you should begin to limit your chosen, general subject but will also suggest a number of possible theses inherent in it.

Sometimes a single sentence or phrase in this article will alert your attention and suggest a question you will want to investigate. In fact, if your chosen subject is at all interesting to you, it would be almost impossible to read any general article without finding phrases or sentences which will challenge you to investigate further some aspect of that subject. Look for ideas that prompt you to ask why or how they are true or in what specific way they may be true. These ideas will provide a basis upon which you will formulate a temporary thesis and a temporary outline (discussed under STEP 3).

If, for example, you are studying French and read a general article about France, you will find countless possibilities for research topics ranging from a comparative study of the French and American revolutions to the study of a particular influence (political, military, economic, religious) upon the French character. If you are studying world literature and decide to write about Anton Chekhov (because you once enjoyed seeing one of his plays), you might be alerted by any of the following statements: he contributed to the comic papers in Russia during the 1880s; he visited a convict island named Sakhalin and wrote a book about it which effected changes in the regime of that penal colony; his stories are developed along "calculated curves"; his masterpiece, *My Life,* is filled with symbols that give it an almost religious character. Such statements should arouse your curiosity, make you want to know more about some particular aspect of Chekhov's work, and send you searching for information that might substantiate any thesis you finally decide to develop. Certainly, such ideas should point out many fascinating paths for you to explore.

Any time you browse through an encyclopedia, you will find wonderful surprises and delightful reading which may prove to be "an arch wherethro' gleams that untravelled world" of knowledge and understanding which awaits all students. Some subject you once thought or heard about but never had a chance to pursue may challenge you to look into its various implications. Even a cursory reading of almost any general article will certainly prove that your problem will never be one of not finding some idea to research; your only problem will be deciding which of the myriad facets of life you will choose to investigate and then reveal in your research project. No matter what thesis suggests itself as you read an encyclopedia article, your pursuit of it will enable you to take a giant step toward an increased perception, awareness, and enjoyment of the all-too-often hidden world around you.

STEP

FORMULATE A TEMPORARY THESIS AND A TEMPORARY OUTLINE

After you have found a general subject and have read a general article for background, you must next decide how you will work with the topic you have chosen. You might, for example, have selected an author as the subject of your paper. You will have access to books and articles which deal with facts about his personal life, his work, his environment, the influences on his life and work, and the significance of his influence on others. Certainly, there would be no value in simply restating the facts and opinions as you have read them; you could not retell them all, and you would have no criterion for deciding how to select those that you would retell. Consequently, you will have to decide to concentrate on some point which your preliminary reading has suggested is a truth about your topic and which further reading would probably substantiate and clarify. Just as the creative artist is led to make a final statement of truth about some aspect of life by observing and selecting from the myriad details of life's experiences, so you, as a researcher, must be able to crystallize a statement of truth by observing and selecting meaningful details from the wealth of material you will find on your topic. This truth, stated in a simple sentence, provides you with a temporary thesis. It is a statement of your opinion, a conclusion which, from what you have read, you have reason to believe is true, but which you are scholar enough to discard or alter later if you uncover facts that prove it invalid. A good thesis is never the statement of a preconceived notion or a personal prejudice that you could prove only by distorting or ignoring facts, nor is it the statement of any indisputable fact about which further investigation would reveal nothing.

If, for example, you wanted to do your research on some area of mythology, you might find, in the course of reading, that you cannot understand the implications of the dismemberment of Osiris. This discovery would not, however, justify a thesis statement that states that most myths are just stories that have no meaning. (Such a thesis would be a preconceived notion showing the limitation of your own understanding). Neither would you consider a thesis statement saying that many primitive societies developed their own mythologies (an indisputable fact). However, because you might have read that the same imagery is often found in the myths of geographically separated and diverse cultures, you might consider an investigation of the similarities and differences in the meaning of some particular images as they appear among different peoples in different areas of the world; you would try to find out whether the images had the same significance or were connected to the same sorts of rituals. Perhaps as a result of reading in the general article that there are many similarities between African creation myths and myths concerning death, you might be challenged to investigate the relationship between creativity (fertility) and death in the mythology of the Korumba people of Africa. On the other hand, you might have been alerted by a statement in a general article that a particular Mexican mask is used in a ritual that "acts out" the story of a myth about Quetzalcoatl and decide to show how the details of the mythology are translated into the specific actions of the ritual. You might also find out how and why these actions are included in some areas and omitted from the reenactment elsewhere. In other words, you will investigate one aspect of what you have read to ascertain its validity. As you question and search in your reading and note taking for the answers to your questions, you will reevaluate your facts and modify your first opinion until you are closer to the ultimate truth, the discovery of which is always the purpose of your research.

It is important to limit your temporary thesis as soon as possible so that, within the limits of the time in which you have to work and the assigned length of the finished paper, the truth of that thesis statement can be investigated thoroughly. The more minutely and specifically the road is marked, the more likely it is that you and your reader will reach the same destination: the realization of the truth of your thesis. No factor is more often responsible for the poor research paper than is the failure to limit a thesis. It is obvious that the less area you try to cover, the more depth you can explore and the more valuable your finished paper will be.

After attending an exhibition of ancient Egyptian art and reading the catalog from it, you might realize how valuable it would be to know something about Egyptian mythology; you might even wonder whether there is a strong relationship between art and mythology in other primitive cultures. That question could challenge you to formulate a thesis that involved a study of the relationship of art and mythology in primitive cultures in general. However, you would see very quickly that, because of the innumerable perspectives from which art and mythology can be compared, there are too many possibilities for development in one paper. Therefore, you might scan the material that covers the various thematic concerns of mythology to see whether what you have read in the general article concerning Egyptian art suggests a basic but limited area for a comparative study. You might find, for example, that creation myths constitute a very large group of myths in most cultures. Therefore, by reading a general article about primitve art, you might note that much of this art attempts to express visually the mythology of "the beginning." A comparative study of the two modes of expression would now give you a basis upon which to narrow and reformulate your temporary thesis. Although this thesis is necessarily a temporary one because you have not accumulated all the available facts yet, it does provide you with an angle of vision from which you can continue your research. You now know how you are going to focus on your subject.

The particular angle of vision you have chosen will automatically suggest and determine the temporary outline you must work with. If you formulate a thesis stating that humanity's attempt to understand the basic phenomena of life is expressed metaphorically both verbally in mythology and visually in art, you would be compelled to investigate the truth of that statement (1) by finding out how and to what extent mythology and art are metaphorically expressed, (2) by discovering what baisc phenomena of life are expressed both visually and verbally, and (3) by considering how and to what extent the visual and verbal expression are comparable in expressing the attitudes and beliefs of their respective cultures. You may not be certain that you can find a sufficient basis for comparison, but it is obvious from the outset that these three questions, which constitute the points of your temporary outline, must be investigated before you can conclusively state your thesis as truth. Similarly, a logical analysis of any thesis that you choose to work with will suggest the points that provide your temporary outline. They outline the path through which you and your reader must travel before the statement you first wrote as a temporary thesis can be stated as a valid conclusion and become your final thesis.

With the formulation of your thesis as a temporary objective and with an outline statement of the points by which you can logically reach it, you have the necessary criteria by which, with a minimum of wasted effort, to select books for your bibliography (STEP 4) and to choose information for your notecards (STEP 5).

In setting up your temporary outline, you are actually using a deductive process. You have temporarily accepted a general statement, or premise, and you are going to investigate your sources to see whether or not that premise can be substantially supported by facts. Because a generality is completely meaningless unless it is supported by specific evidence, it is extremely important that you use the most authoritative sources available in which to find your facts. You must be wary of unsigned editorial columns or magazine articles that are not carefully documented. It is for this reason, also, that you must consult many different sources representing a wide range of thinking in order to make your paper valuable as research. However, in spite of the fact that your temporary outline is the result of a deductive process, your final thesis and outline must be inductively developed. That is, you must eventually analyze your material, or the facts accumulated, and change your temporary thesis, so that it is ultimately stated as an accurate result or conclusion of the material *you* have observed and presented. The temporary thesis, then, was the statement of a hunch or of an educated guess; the final thesis is the result of research and is a statement of truth. It is the only conclusion to which one could come from the material that *you* have selected and presented.

STEP

PREPARE THE PRELIMINARY BIBLIOGRAPHY

WHY A PRELIMINARY BIBLIOGRAPHY IS NECESSARY

There are several reasons why, before you begin to do your research, it is important to prepare a preliminary bibliography even though it will include books you will never see or use.

1. You must be sure that adequate information on the subject is available to you and that your thesis is not hackneyed.

2. You must allow time to order any pertinent published materials which you may need to obtain through the interlibrary loan service. There is a nominal charge for postage, and you should be prepared to wait at least a week.

3. You need to become familiar with the type of research that has been done on your topic.

4. From seeing a variety of titles, you will learn how your chosen thesis might be further limited or broadened.

5. You will be given clues about titles, subjects, and authors relating to your particular subject; for example, in looking up *Mythology,* you will find a section on *Creation Myths* which would lead you to *Types of Creation Myths* or *Origins of Creation Myths* as well as *Theories of Creation Myths* and thence to the specific names of mythologists who have much to say about creation myths, such as Sir James Frazer or Joseph Campbell.

WHERE TO FIND A PRELIMINARY BIBLIOGRAPHY

There are many places where you will find a listing of materials that you can include in your preliminary bibliography. Of course, your bibliography will change considerably before it becomes final because many of the titles you find in your preliminary search will not be available, some will not be useful, and new sources will be added constantly as you read. Do not look in only one place for your sources. Try to investigate each of the following sections in the libraries available to you.*

1. The Card Catalog

Check to see how the materials in your library are cataloged. Some libraries have a single catalog in which you can look up author, title, or subject, all arranged in alphabetical order. Other libraries have a separate author catalog in which you can locate the card for a book if you know the author's name; a second catalog then contains alphabetized titles and subjects. Depending on your subject and your knowledge of it, you will look for books under a particular subject, a particular author, or a particular title. The author card for any book is considered the basic entry card. It is therefore important for you to know the significance of each entry on it

---

*See The Library, pp. 108-111. See also Reference Materials and Guides, pp. 117-122.

Example of an Author Card in the Card Catalog

```
BL      Campbell, Joseph, 1904–
315        Myths to live by. Foreword by
C27        Johnson E. Fairchild. New York,
           Viking Press [1972]
             x, 276 p. 22 cm.

           Based on thirteen lectures
           delivered at the Cooper Union Forum
           between 1958 and 1971.

             1. Mythology–Addresses, essays,
           lectures. I. Title.

BL315.C27                      398'.042
           LSLB                78–181974

ISBN 0–670–50359–2 A7–837283 A          MARC
```

NOTES:

This card, like all author cards, identifies the book by the call number* in the upper left-hand corner.

The author's name is given in inverted order; the dates of birth and death are often included.

The first letter of the first word in each title is capitalized; but often, the entire title of the book is neither capitalized nor italicized on the catalog card. You must remember to capitalize the first and last words and then all other words of the title except for CAPs (conjunctions, articles, and prepositions); also remember to underline each word of the title separately to indicate italics.

If a bibliography is included in the book, the card will indicate it.

The Library of Congress number is the call number here; it will be at the bottom of a card using the Dewey decimal system classification.

This book is cataloged also under its titles (after Roman numerals), its subjects (after the Arabic numbers), and if there were an editor and a translator they would be also listed after Roman numerals. The Dewey

---

*See Library Classification Systems, pp. 115–117.

decimal call number follows the Library of Congress number at the bottom.

The way in which any book is cataloged or cross-filed will suggest other possible subjects for you to investigate.

2. Periodical Indexes

These will list magazine articles published on your subject; some of the most important indexes are listed below.

a. *The Reader's Guide to Periodical Literature* will list articles published in American magazines since 1900. It is a subject and author index with cross references; however, the subject index is the more complete.

NOTE: You will have to look in the volume for each year in which articles on your subject could have been written; for example, you would not look up *atomic energy* in the 1930 volume, but you would look up *mythology* in every volume.

Do not put the information on your bibliography card the way it appears in *The Reader's Guide*. The abbreviations are explained at the front of each volume. The entry in the 1980 volume, which appears thus:

The Aztecs. B. McDowell. Nat Geog 158:704-52 Dec '80

will be translated to a bibliography card thus:

```
McDowell, Bart.
"The Aztecs."
National Geographic,
December, 1980,
pp. 704-752.
```

b. (1) *Social Science Index* (1907 to date), and

(2) *Humanities Index* (1907 to date) cover many learned and professional journals not included in *The Reader's Guide* and list foreign as well as American periodicals. They are extremely valuable for articles published since 1907. It is important to note that until 1974 these two indexes were combined into one index. That single index was titled *The International Index to Periodical Literature* from 1907-1966. In 1966 its name changed to *Social Science and*

Humanities Index. This lasted until 1974, when it was separated into the two indexes that now exist.

c. *Poole's Index to Periodical Literature* is a subject index to British and American magazine articles published from 1802-1906.

d. *Nineteenth Century Reader's Guide to Periodical Literature* (1890-1899) is an index to fifty-one periodicals from 1890-1899. It gives the subject, author, and illustrator; some works of literature are listed under title entries. A special feature is the identification (wherever possible) of articles published anonymously.

e. *Book Review Digest* (1905 to date) gives reports on contemporary reviews and brief but useful information about the worth of books. There are excerpts from many of the reviews cited.

f. *MLA Bibliographies* (1921 to present) are yearly volumes listing essays in various periodicals devoted to language and literature (English, American, French, Spanish, Italian, German).

3. Special Indexes

These include listings of books and magazines and newspaper articles on a variety of special subjects (such as education, religion, art, book reviews, medicine, engineering, biographies) and are usually found on open reference-room shelves. For example,

The New York Times Index classifies all of the *Times* articles. It gives the date on which an event occurred, making it easier for you to look up information in other newspapers; its obituaries contain valuable biographical material about prominent people.

Essay and General Literature Index lists more of the scholarly magazine articles on more sophisticated subjects than *The Reader's Guide.*

PMLA (the journal called *Publications of the Modern Language Association*) has an index in each May issue.

4. Bibliographies

There are many publications which are themselves merely bibliographies. Some are compiled on particular subjects; others, on a particular person and his work. For example,

Sheehy, Eugene Paul, comp. *Guide to Reference Books,* 9th ed. (1976; Supplement, 1980), divides his bibliography by subject

(General Reference Works, The Humanities, Social Sciences, History and Area Studies, Pure and Applied Sciences); under each subject are numerous subcategories, each containing still more categories. Such an arrangement makes it possible to locate reference material on any subject easily and accurately.

Mark, Linda, ed. *Reference Sources,* 3 vols. (1979), divides her bibliography alphabetically according to the last name of the author and "provides indexing to all reference books which have been reviewed in over 140 journals." She lists "dictionaries, bibliographies, atlases, gazetteers, biographical dictionaries, chronologies, thesauri, indexes, statistical tables, directories" as well as "art catalogs (especially the catalog raisonné) and annual 'state of the art' reviews."

There are more indexes listed on pp. 117-122.

5. Special Encyclopedias

Many of these include excellent bibliographies in addition to the articles on particular subjects. For example, you will find bibliographies at the end of most articles in the *Encyclopaedia Britannica.* Check the card catalog for encyclopedias on special subjects, such as art, American history, American government, religion, physics, music, and so forth.

6. Sources Which You Use

In most of your sources you will find clues to other relevant material by looking either in a bibliography at the back, in the footnotes, or in the material itself.

HOW TO WRITE YOUR BIBLIOGRAPHY CARDS

Record each entry or source on a separate 3 × 5 inch index card.

Record the name of the author, the title, and the facts of publication accurately. The card, not the book, will be the source of information for the data you will use later in writing the footnotes and the final bibliography.

In order to save time and effort, you should make up your cards with whatever information you have, leaving lines and spaces to be completed when you have the actual book or other source in your hands.

On the back of the bibliography card put the call number and/or the place where you found out about this source. Also put any other information to which you might want to refer later.

There are only two basic bibliographical forms:

1. There is a basic form for a source with its own title.

2. There is a basic form for an article contained within a larger work.

FORM FOR A SOURCE WITH ITS OWN TITLE

(Note: You need not have used or read the entire work.)

```
Campbell, Joseph.
Myths to Live By.
New York: The Viking Press,
1972.
```

1st line: author's name in inverted order

(If there are two or more authors, use the form in example 3 or 4 below.)

end punctuation: period

2nd line: title of book

(Capitalize the first and last word and all other words except CAPs—short conjunctions, articles, and short prepositions; underline each word separately to indicate title as it appears on outside of book; underlining is a substitute for italics.)

end punctuation: period

3rd line: facts of publication

Place of publication followed by colon and name of publisher.

end punctuation: comma

NOTES: You must write the name of the publisher exactly as it appears on the title page, abbreviating and capitalizing only those words that are abbreviated and/or capitalized.

If more than one place of publication is given, use the first one listed unless it is in a foreign country; if only a foreign country is given, use it.

If the publisher is not given, write the abbreviation in brackets thus: [n.p.].

If the place of publication is not given, write the abbreviation in brackets thus: [n.p.].

4th line: date of publication

(Whenever more than one date of publication or copyright is given, use the most recent one. If no date is given, write the abbreviation in brackets thus: [n.d.].)

end punctuation: period

Models for a source with its own title

1. the basic form

```
Campbell, Joseph.
Myths to Live By.
New York: The Viking Press,
1972.
```

2. no author

```
Máscaras Mexicanas: de la Colección
   del Ing. Victor José Moya.
Mexico City: Dirección de Museos del
   Instituto Nacional de Antropología
   e Historia,
1974.
```

3. two authors

```
Burland, C. A., and Werner Forman.
Feathered Serpent and Smoking Mirror.
New York: G. P. Putnam's Sons,
1975.
```

4. more than two authors

```
López Portillo, José, and others.
Quetzalcoatl.
Mexico City: Secretaría de
  Asentamientos Humanos y Obras
  Públicas,
1977.
```

NOTE: The author line may be thus:
    López Portillo, José, et al.
    (the author's full name is José López Portillo).

5. corporate authorship

```
Committee on College Teaching.
College Teaching as a Career.
Washington, D.C.: American Council
  on Education,
1958.
```

6. an author and an editor

```
Wordsworth, William.
The Prelude or Growth of a Poet's Mind.
Ed. Ernest de Selincourt.
New York: Oxford University Press,
1947.
```

7. an author and a translator

```
Eliade, Mircea.
Images and Symbols.
Trans. Philip Mairet.
Kansas City, Missouri: Sheed Andrews
  and McMeel,
1961.
```

8. an author, an editor, and a translator

```
Neruda, Pablo.
A New Decade (Poems: 1958–1967).
Ed. Ben Belitt.
Trans. Ben Belitt and Alastair Reid.
New York: Grove Press,
1969.
```

9. an editor but no author

```
Mitchell, W. J. T., ed.
The Language of Images.
Chicago: The University of Chicago Press,
1980.
```

NOTE: This form would be used when referring to an anthology as a whole rather than one of the works included in the anthology as well as for any other book with an editor but no author.

10. a compiler

```
Muser, Curt, comp.
Facts and Artifacts of Ancient
  Middle America.
New York: E. P. Dutton,
1978.
```

11. one volume in a multivolume set when all volumes have the same title

```
Budge, E. A. Wallis.
The Gods of the Egyptians or Studies
  in Egyptian Mythology, Vol. II. 2 vols.
1904;
rpt. New York: Dover Publications,
1969.
```

NOTE: This is a modern reprint of a book originally published in 1904. See example 16.

12. one volume in a multivolume set when each volume has a separate title

```
Russell, John.
The Dominion of the Dream.
Vol. VII of The Meanings of Modern Art.
  11 vols.
New York: The Museum of Modern Art,
1975.
```

13. a book in a series edited by one other than the author

```
Maclagen, David.
Creation Myths: Man's Introduction to
  the World.
In the Art and Imagination series.
Ed. Jill Purce.
London: Thames and Hudson,
1977.
```

NOTE: If the volumes were numbered, the third line would be thus:
Vol. II of Art and Imagination, as in example 12.

14. a book with a subtitle or secondary title

```
Hopper, Vincent F., ed. and trans.
Chaucer's Canterbury Tales: An Interlinear
  Translation.
Woodbury, New York: Barron's,
1970.
```

NOTE: Obviously Chaucer did not write a book with this title; therefore this
entry is correct for this book. If you quoted the introduction by Dr.
Hopper, you would use this card for bibliography and for footnote. If
you quoted the lines from Chaucer with the older spelling, your card
would be thus:

14a.

```
Chaucer, Geoffrey.
"The Pardoner's Tale."
Chaucer's Canterbury Tales: An Interlinear
  Translation.
Ed. and trans. Vincent F. Hopper.
Woodbury, New York: Barron's,
1970.
```

15. an edition subsequent to the first edition

```
Parrinder, Geoffrey.
African Traditional Religion, 3rd ed.
New York: Harper and Row,
1976.
```

16. a modern reprint of an older edition

```
Toor, Frances.
Mexican Popular Arts.
1939;
rpt. Detroit: Blaine Ethridge Books,
1973.
```

17. a pamphlet, bulletin, or manual

```
Halpin, Marjorie M.
Viewing Objects in Series: The Raven
   Rattle (UBC Museum of Anthropology
   Note No. 6).
Vancouver: University of British Columbia
   Museum of Anthropology,
1978.
```

NOTE: Omit parenthetical entry if the pamphlet is not one of a series.

18. a catalog of an exhibition

Brown, Betty Ann, curator.
Máscaras: Dance Masks of Mexico and
  Guatemala (an exhibit at the Ewing
  Museum of Nations, Illinois State
  University, April 21–December 16, 1978).
Bloomington, Illinois: University Museums,
  Illinois State University,
1978.

19. a government document

U. S., Congressional Record,
80th Cong., 2nd Sess., 1948,
XCII, Part 6, 5539.

20. a dictionary

Webster's New Collegiate Dictionary.
Springfield, Massachusetts: G. & C.
  Merriam Company,
1976.

21. a record or tape

Liszt, Franz.
Late Piano Works (Alfred Brendel,
  piano).
Philips, 9500 775.

22. a film

Romeo and Juliet.
Franco Zeffirelli, director-producer.
Paramount Pictures,
1968.

23. a radio program

The Art of Hilde Gueden.
KUSC (91.5 FM), Los Angeles.
10:00 am, July 1, 1981.

24. a television program

Hidden Places: Where History Lives, pt. I.
KCET (Channel 28), Los Angeles.
9:30 pm, August 7, 1981.

FORM FOR A SOURCE CONTAINED WITHIN A LARGER WORK

McDowell, Bart.
"The Aztecs."
National Geographic,
December, 1980,
pp. 704–752.

1st line: author's name in reverse order

(For two or more authors, see examples 3 and 4 in the section above.)

end punctuation: period

2nd line: title of the article, essay, or poem (the contained work) **capitalized (first letter of each word) and enclosed in quotation marks**

end punctuation: period before the closing quotation marks

(If there is punctuation as part of the title, enclose that punctuation within the quotation marks as part of the title and omit your period.)

3rd line: title of the larger work in which the article appears

(The title is underlined, one word at a time, and first letter of each word is capitalized except for CAPs—short conjunctions, articles, and short prepositions.)

The title is followed by a comma; if your instructor insists on a volume number, give it in Roman numerals alone (without the abbreviation for *volume*), followed by a comma.

end punctuation: comma (if no parentheses will follow on line 4)
                          no comma (if parentheses will follow on line 4)

4th line: the date of publication followed by a comma:

December, 1980,

OR if you put a volume number on line 3, then put parentheses around the date with a comma after the closing mark:

(December, 1980),

5th line: the pages on which the particular article can be found

(If line 3 had a volume given, omit the abbreviation p. or pp.; if no volume is given on line 3, there will be no parentheses on line 4 and you will use the abbreviations p. or pp.)

end punctuation: period

(To give the pages on which an article occurs, use
p. 12 to indicate that the article is complete on one page;
pp. 11-19 to indicate that the article covers nine pages;
pp. 11-19, 36 to indicate that after the first nine pages, the article continues
          on p. 36;
pp. 11-19, 36-40 to indicate that after the first nine pages, the article
          continues from pages 36 to 40.)

Models for a source contained within a larger work

1. the basic form

```
McDowell, Bart.
"The Aztecs."
National Geographic,
December, 1980,
pp. 704-752.
```

2. a magazine article with no author

```
"The Trajectories of Genius."
Time,
May 26, 1980,
p. 79.
```

3. an untitled book review

```
Cole, Herbert M.
Review of Two Thousand Years of
  Nigerian Art, by Ekpo Eyo.
African Arts,
February, 1979,
pp. 16-19, 80-81.
```

NOTE: If this review had had a title, it would have been given in quotation marks on the line after the name of the reviewer, Cole; the entry would then continue as above.

4. a newspaper article or editorial

```
Drake, Sylvie.
"Santa Fe: Artists in the Desert."
Los Angeles Times,
August 5, 1981,
VI; 1, 5.
```

NOTE: For an unsigned article, you would write nothing on the top line; the last line indicates that the article is in section VI and that it begins on page 1 and is continued on page 5; note that when both a section (or volume) number and page numbers are given, neither the abbreviation *sec.* for section (or *vol.* for volume) nor *pp.* for pages is used.

5. an essay (or other article) written by one person in an anthology edited by another

```
Argan, Giulio Carlo.
"Ideology and Iconology."
The Language of Images.
Ed. W. J. T. Mitchell.
Chicago: The University of Chicago Press,
1980.
Pp. 15-23.
```

6. an encyclopedia article

```
Dundes, Alan.
"Myth: Myths of the Beginning and of the End."
Encyclopaedia Britannica (1970),
XV, 1135-1138.
```

NOTE: Most articles are signed with only the initials of the author; at the front of the first volume is a list of the initials and full names of the contributors.

As in example 4 above, both the abbreviations vol. and pp. have been omitted.

For an unsigned article, you would write nothing on the first line above the title of the article; leave the line blank because you may find the name of the author later.

Encyclopedias reverse titles and names in order to list articles alphabetically; you may or may not, but be consistent.

7. an introduction or limited part of a book by one other than the author

```
Furst, Peter T.
"Foreword" to
Donald Cordry, Mexican Masks.
Austin, Texas: University of Texas Press,
1980.
Pp. ix-xx.
```

8. author of part of a book in a series edited by others

```
Mason, Herbert.
"Myth as an 'Ambush of Reality.' "
Myth, Symbol, and Reality.
Ed. Alan M. Olson.
Vol. I of the Boston University Studies in
   Philosophy and Religion.
Ed. Leroy S. Rouner.
Notre Dame, Indiana: University of Notre
   Dame Press,
1980.
Pp. 15-19.
```

9. a reprint with critical comment by the editor

```
Wright, Andrew.
"Afterword" in
Joyce Cary, The Horse's Mouth.
1944;
rpt. New York: Perennial Library—Harper and Row,
1965.
Pp. 347–353.
```

10. a casebook (a text for controlled research)

```
Stevenson, David.
"J. D. Salinger: The Mirror of Crisis."
The Nation,
March 9, 1957,
pp. 215–217;
rpt. If You Really Want to Know: A Catcher
  Casebook.
Ed. Malcolm M. Marsden.
Chicago: Scott, Foresman,
1963.
Pp. 22–25.
```

NOTE: There are two ways to use a casebook: as an anthology of essays about a particular subject or as a library containing essays which you will read and document as if you were reading the original. For the latter use, the original pagination appears in the casebook with slash marks wherever a page change occurred in the original. Check with your instructor about how to use the casebook; but it would never be wrong to use the form above.

FORMS FOR SPECIAL PROBLEMS

1. an interview

```
Markman, Roberta H.
Professor of Comparative Literature,
  California State University,
Personal interview on Mexican masks.
Long Beach, California,
April 16, 1980.
```

NOTE: Unless the person interviewed is well known, you should indicate through the use of the person's title why he or she is an authority on the subject of the interview.

2. an unpublished lecture

```
Markman, Peter T.
Professor of English, Fullerton College.
Class Lecture on Carlos Fuentes, The
  Death of Artemio Cruz.
Fullerton, California,
May 3, 1981.
```

3. a published lecture

```
Vonnegut, Kurt Jr.
"Address to Graduating Class at Bennington
  College, 1970."
Wampeters, Foma and Granfalloons (Opinions).
New York: Dell,
1976.
Pp. 159–168.
```

4. mimeographed material

```
Brown, Betty Ann.
"Fiestas de Oaxaca."
1977.                    (mimeographed)
```

NOTE: Try to give as much identifying information as you can for material of this nature.

5. an unpublished thesis or dissertation

```
Markman, Roberta H.
"Mann's Joseph: From Dreamer to Artist."
Unpublished Ph.D. dissertation,
Dept. of Comparative Literature,
  Occidental College, Los Angeles,
1969.
```

6. a letter

```
Hemingway, Ernest.
A letter to Roberta Hoffman, dated August 12,
  1957, New York, and now in the archives of
  The University of Texas at El Paso Library,
  El Paso, Texas.
```

NOTE: In a footnote, simply: Unpublished letter from Ernest Hemingway to Roberta Hoffman, August 12, 1957.

7. the Bible or any well-known literary work which can be identified by book or scene plus lines or by chapter and verse

```
a. I Corinthians.
   The Bible.
   Revised Standard Version.
```

NOTE: The names of sacred scripture are neither underlined nor put in quotation marks. The translation of the Bible is assumed to be the King James Version unless another is named, as in the example above.

```
b. Milton, John.
   Paradise Lost.
   Book I.
```

NOTE: The particular edition you used is not needed unless the work is a translation.

The name of a novel, a play, or a long poem would be underlined even if it is part of an anthology.

8. an abridgment

```
Style Manual (abridged), rev. ed.
Washington, D.C.: Government Printing Office,
1959.
```

9. record jacket information

The Bitter and the Sweet.
Pete Seeger.
Columbia Records, CS 8716,
1962.
Jacket notes.

10. a pamphlet included with a record

Kostelanetz, Richard, and Editors of
  Time—Life Records.
"A Listener's Guide to the Recordings."
The Music of Today.
In The Story of Great Music series.
Time—Life Records, STL 145.

11. a lecture on a record or tape

Scherman, Thomas, narrator and conductor.
"Musical Program Notes."
Beethoven's Symphony No. 5 in C Minor,
  Op. 67 (Sir Adrian Boult conducting
  The Philharmonic Promenade Orchestra of
  London).
Vanguard, MARS 3005.

HOW TO PREPARE
THE FINAL BIBLIOGRAPHY
(TO BE DONE AS PART OF STEP 10)

1. Take out all the bibliography cards to which you have referred in your footnotes. These cards constitute your working bibliography and are the only ones which will be used in making your final bibliography.

2. The number of sources you will list on the final bibliography should equal the number of first-entry footnotes in your paper. (These are the footnotes which give full bibliographical information the first time you document material from a source.)

3. Alphabetize your working bibliography cards according to the first letter that appears on the card, excepting *a, an,* and *the.* (The first letter may be in the author's name, the title of a magazine article, and so forth.) If the title begins with a Roman numeral, alphabetize according to the word that follows the Roman numeral; if the first word in the title is an Arabic number, alphabetize according to the way that number would be spelled. For example, "X Steps" would be alphabetized under *S,* but "10 Steps" would be alphabetized under *T.*

4. Since the bibliography page is a title page, the title, BIBLIOGRAPHY, is centered and typed in capitals without underlining, and the page number is centered at the bottom of the page; it may be enclosed by parentheses or dashes.

5. The bibliography entries are single-spaced within each entry and double-spaced between entries. Write as a continuous sentence; do not divide into lines as on the cards. The second and subsequent lines of each entry are indented as for a paragraph (five spaces); the punctuation on the bibliography card is copied exactly.

6. Bibliography entries are never numbered. Ordinarily, the bibliography is not divided into types of sources.

BIBLIOGRAPHY*

Argan, Giulio Carlo. "Ideology and Iconology." The Language of Images. Ed. W. J. T. Mitchell. The University of Chicago Press, 1980. Pp. 15–23.

The Art of Hilde Gueden. KUSC (91.5 FM), Los Angeles. 10:00 am, July 1, 1981.

The Bitter and the Sweet. Pete Seeger. Columbia Records, CS 8716, 1962. Jacket notes.

Brown, Betty Ann. "Fiestas de Oaxaca." 1977. (Mimeographed.)

†_____, curator. Máscaras: Dance Masks of Mexico and Guatemala (an exhibit at the Ewing Museum of Nations, Illinois State University, April 21–December 16, 1978). Bloomington, Illinois: University Museums, Illinois State University, 1978.

Budge, E. A. Wallis. The Gods of the Egyptians or Studies in Egyptian Mythology, Vol. II. 2 vols. 1904; rpt. New York: Dover Publications, 1969.

Burland, C. A., and Werner Forman. Feathered Serpent and Smoking Mirror. New York: G. P. Putnam's Sons, 1975.

Campbell, Joseph. Myths to Live By. New York: The Viking Press, 1972.

Chaucer, Geoffrey. "The Pardoner's Tale." Chaucer's Canterbury Tales: An Interlinear Translation. Ed. and trans. Vincent F. Hopper. Woodbury, New York: Barron's, 1970.

Cole, Herbert M. Review of Two Thousand Years of Nigerian Art, by Ekpo Eyo. African Arts, February, 1979, pp. 16–19, 80–81.

Committee on College Teaching. College Teaching as a Career. Washington, D.C.: American Council on Education, 1958.

NOTE: All of these sources are reproduced as footnotes beginning on page 72.

---

*This is a sample bibliography compiled from the sample bibliography cards shown on the preceding pages.

† This line indicates that the author for this entry is the same as for the entry immediately above. Underline seven spaces before the punctuation mark.

I Corinthians. The Bible. Revised Standard Version.

Drake, Sylvie. "Santa Fe: Artists in the Desert." Los Angeles Times, August 5, 1981, VI; 1, 5.

Dundes, Alan. "Myth: Myths of the Beginning and of the End." Encyclopaedia Britannica (1970), XV, 1135–1138.

Eliade, Mircea. Images and Symbols. Trans. Philip Mairet. Kansas City, Missouri: Sheed Andrews and McMeel, 1961.

Furst, Peter T. "Foreword" to Donald Cordry, Mexican Masks. Austin, Texas: University of Texas Press, 1980. Pp. ix–xx.

Halpin, Marjorie M. Viewing Objects in Series: The Raven Rattle (UBC Museum of Anthropology Note No. 6). Vancouver: University of British Columbia Museum of Anthropology, 1978.

Hemingway, Ernest. A letter to Roberta Hoffman, dated August 12, 1957, New York, and now in the archives of The University of Texas at El Paso Library, El Paso, Texas.

Hidden Places: Where History Lives, pt. I. KCET (Channel 28), Los Angeles. 9:30 pm, August 7, 1981.

Hopper, Vincent F. ed. and trans. Chaucer's Canterbury Tales: An Interlinear Translation. Woodbury, New York: Barron's, 1970.

Kostelanetz, Richard, and Editors of Time–Life Records. "A Listener's Guide to the Recordings." The Music of Today. In The Story of Great Music series. Time–Life Records, STL 145.

Liszt, Franz. Late Piano Works (Alfred Brendel, piano). Philips, 9500 775.

Lopez Portillo, José, and others. Quetzalcoatl. Mexico City: Secretaría de Asentamientos Humanos y Obras Públicas, 1977.

Maclagen, David. Creation Myths: Man's Introduction to the World. In the Art and Imagination series. Ed. Jill Purce. London: Thames and Hudson, 1977.

Markman, Peter T. Professor of English, Fullerton College. Class Lecture on Carlos Fuentes, The Death of Artemio Cruz. Fullerton College, Fullerton, California, May 3, 1981.

Markman, Roberta H. "Mann's Joseph: From Dreamer to Artist." Unpublished Ph.D. dissertation, Dept. of Comparative Literature, Occidental College, Los Angeles, 1969.

————. Professor of Comparative Literature, California State University, Long Beach. Personal interview on Mexican masks. Long Beach, California, April 16, 1980.

Máscaras Mexicanas: de la Colección del Ing. Victor José Moya. Mexico City: Dirección de Museos del Instituto Nacional de Antropología e Historia, 1974.

Mason, Herbert. "Myth as an 'Ambush of Reality.'" Myth, Symbol, and Reality. Ed. Alan M. Olson. Vol. I of the Boston University Studies in Philosophy and Religion. Ed. Leroy S. Rouner. Notre Dame, Indiana: University of Notre Dame Press, 1980. Pp. 15–19.

McDowell, Bart. "The Aztecs." National Geographic, December, 1980, pp. 704–752.

Milton, John. Paradise Lost. Book I.

Mitchell, W. J. T., ed. The Language of Images. Chicago: The University of Chicago Press, 1980.

Muser, Curt, comp. Facts and Artifacts of Ancient Middle America. New York: E. P. Dutton, 1978.

Neruda, Pablo. A New Decade (Poems: 1958–1967). Ed. Ben Belitt. Trans. Ben Belitt and Alastair Reid. New York: Grove Press, 1969.

Parrinder, Geoffrey. African Traditional Religion, 3rd ed. New York: Harper & Row, 1976.

Romeo and Juliet. Franco Zeffirelli, director-producer. Paramount Pictures, 1968.

Russell, John. The Dominion of the Dream. Vol. VII of The Meanings of Modern Art. 11 vols. New York: The Museum of Modern Art, 1975.

Scherman, Thomas, narrator and conductor. "Musical Program Notes." Beethoven's Symphony No. 5 in C Minor, Op. 67 (Sir Adrian Boult conducting The Philharmonic Promenade Orchestra of London). Vanguard, MARS 3005.

Stevenson, David. "J. D. Salinger: The Mirror of Crisis." The Nation, March 9, 1957, pp. 215–217; rpt. If You Really Want to Know: A Catcher Casebook. Ed. Malcolm M. Marsden. Chicago: Scott, Foresman, 1963. Pp. 22–25.

Style Manual (abridged), rev. ed. Washington, D.C.: Government Printing Office, 1959.

Toor, Frances. Mexican Popular Arts. 1939; rpt. Detroit: Blaine Ethridge Books, 1973.

"The Trajectories of Genius." Time, May 26, 1980, p. 79.

U. S., Congressional Record, 80th Cong., 2nd Sess., 1948, XCII, Part 6, 5539.

Vonnegut, Kurt Jr. "Address to Graduating Class at Bennington College, 1970." Wampeters, Foma and Granfalloons (Opinions). New York: Dell, 1976. Pp. 159–168.

Webster's New Collegiate Dictionary. Springfield, Massachusetts: G. & C. Merriam Company, 1976.

Wordsworth, William. The Prelude or Growth of a Poet's Mind. Ed. Ernest de Selincourt. New York: Oxford University Press, 1947.

Wright, Andrew. "Afterword" in Joyce Cary, The Horse's Mouth. 1944; rpt. New York: Perennial Library–Harper and Row, 1965. Pp. 347–353.

STEP

5

TAKE NOTES
FROM RELEVANT
SOURCES

Good notecards are the key to a well-developed, easy-to-read paper and will facilitate the actual writing of your paper. In fact, to a great extent, the notecards actually determine the course of your research and the final paper you will write.

The order in which you take notes will not be the order in which you will use them in your paper; therefore, it is important to keep them independent of each other and clear in meaning to you. Each notecard must be precisely identified as to source and page so that you can document the information if you use it in your paper; or if you are working with sources that are not printed matter, be sure to indicate how and where you obtained your information.

The amount and kind of information you write on each card will vary with the type of note you take, which will be guided not only by the information you record but also by the way you think it might be used in your paper. (The section marked "Kinds of Notecards," pp. 46 to 55 will indicate possible varieties.) Follow the procedure outlined below and your note taking will be orderly and rewarding.

HOW TO TAKE NOTES

1. Write your notes in ink on 4 × 6 inch cards; some instructors may prefer the 3 × 5 inch size.

2. Write on *one* side of the card only; try not to continue an idea on to a second card.

3. Before you take a single note from any source, take out the bibliography card that you have prepared for that source. Check each item of the bibliography card against the source in your hands to make sure that you have the complete and correct facts concerning that particular source. Fill in any information you did not already have on the card.

4. Write an identifying letter symbol very clearly on your bibliography card at the bottom of the card. This letter will identify that particular source as you take notes from it; see the example on the bibliography card (page 45), and on all of the notecards which follow. Be sure not to use any letter twice; only one bibliography card will be marked A, for example, but many notecards may be from the source you identify as A. Go through the alphabet, but do not use the letters I and O, as they could look too much like page numbers. If you have more than 24 sources, double the letters (AA or BB) or add a number (A1, B1), the second time around.

    It is a good idea to keep the bibliography card at hand while you take notes from the source it identifies. Then you can be sure that the letter symbol you enter in the upper left-hand corner of each notecard matches the one on the bibliography card. On a separate "safety sheet" and in a different place, you should keep an alphabetical list of these letters with the complete bibliographical data which each identifies. REMEMBER: The A, B, C symbols will not indicate the order in which you will later list your bibliography (that order will be determined by the first word on the bibliography card) nor will the letters indicate the order in which you take notes or later use the notecards.

NOTE: Many authorities suggest that the author's name be used to identify the source of the notes; others suggest that the abbreviated title be used, and still others prefer that both the title and the author be written on each notecard. However, each of these methods would involve much more time than the use of the identifying letters, and each entails a possible confusion if more than one book or article is written by the same person or has a similar title.

The use of the identifying letter saves much time in inserting documentation on the first draft (see STEP 7), avoids possible confusion of sources, and provides the student with the evidence that every bibliography card so identified has been handled and checked for accuracy of bibliographical data.

5. Write only one idea from one source on each card; never use a single card for notes from two sources.

6. Before you begin to write your notes, be sure to identify the source. In the upper left-hand corner above the top line, write the letter or symbol which identifies the particular source you are now reading. Reserve the rest of the top line for the outline label or slug. See STEP 6.

    Put the page number in a circle before the first word on the notecard. If one idea is discussed on several pages in the source, indicate each page change by encircling the new page number before writing down the first word taken from that page. For example: �36 "There are several factors. . . . �37 The first factor . . . and �40 the second factor are important."

7. Early in your reading you will discover the need to adjust your reading speed to fit the material; not all printed material will be of equal value to you. When Bacon wrote that "some books are to be tasted, others to be swallowed, and some few to be chewed and digested," he could have been writing instructions to the student engaged in research. You must determine the relevance of each new source to your thesis and then decide how you will read it and what notes or information you need to take from it.

8. When you find information which you want, decide which kind of note will suit your needs. Use symbols, signs, and abbreviations to save time in writing the note. Experienced researchers take various kinds of notes, samples of which follow the reproduced sample preface from which all notes in this section are taken.

9. When you are about halfway through your notetaking, see STEP 6 before continuing to take notes.

10. Do not hesitate to take duplicating or contradictory notes; you may need them to defend your thesis later or to have a choice of sources to quote.

NOTE: On each sample notecard in this section, A is the symbol identifying the master's thesis by Markman as the source from which all notes are taken.

Below is the sample bibliography card for that thesis, completed as it would appear when the symbol has been added:

```
Markman, Roberta H.
"The Metaphoric Vision in Mythology and Art."
Unpublished master's thesis,
Department of Comparative Literature, California
  State University, Long Beach,
1982.


                         A
```

The Preface reproduced below is the source for the sample notecards given in the following section.

```
                        PREFACE

    My earliest attraction to mythology was based on a
fascination with the dramatic action of the narratives and
the aura of magic that pervades the world in which that
action takes place. But gradually I realized that on another
level those marvelous tales were metaphorical expressions
of essential aspects of the human condition. Each social
group had obviously developed a mythology by which it could
understand the basic experiences of its existence, such as
creation, nature, and death. Although their mythological
stories might not be literally true, they do by analogy
capture the essential truth both of the society's world view
and of the basic nature of being. Von Franz says that when
man attempts to explain the unknown, he is likely to depend
on imagery from what he does know or on archetypal images
which come out of his own inner experiences.[1] Later I
realized that these images are also found in primitive art.
Mitchell explains that visual representation is "not
radically distinct from language,"[2] and Elizabeth Abel
contends that the underlying concepts of myth and art are
similar in that both express a "common inner source whose
subject matter changes but whose nature is the same."[3] I
```

```
was challenged to investigate the common denominators of
the verbal and visual expressions of these insights and to
do a comparative study of their metaphoric forms.
```

```
    ¹ Marie-Louise von Franz, Patterns of Creativity
Mirrored in Creation Myths (Zürich: Spring Publications,
1978), p. 5. Von Franz bases her conclusions on the images
she has found on maps of antiquity.
    ² W. J. T. Mitchell, "Spatial Form in Literature: Toward
a General Theory," The Language of Images, ed. W. J. T.
Mitchell (Chicago: University of Chicago Press, 1980), p.
296. Mitchell reinforces his point with a quote from Ludwig
Wittgenstein's Philosophical Investigations: "A picture
held us captive. And we could not get outside it, for it lay
in our language and language seemed to repeat it to us
inexorably" (Mitchell, p. 271).
    ³ Elizabeth Abel, "Redefining the Sister Arts:
Baudelaire's Response to the Art of Delacroix," The
Language of Images, ed. W. J. T. Mitchell (Chicago:
University of Chicago Press, 1980), p. 41.
```

```
                              iv
```

Roberta H. Markman, "The Metaphoric Vision in Mythology and Art," (unpublished master's thesis, Department of Comparative Literature, California State University, 1982), p. iv.

KINDS OF NOTECARDS

All notes for the following illustrations are taken from the Preface reproduced on the preceding page. That Preface is part of the master's thesis which is identified on the bibliography card given on page 45 and labeled A; therefore A in the upper left corner of these notecards identifies that source, and (iv) indicates the page number.

A. **Direct quotation (verbatim).** Be accurate; copy from the printed page exactly. Do not change the punctuation or the spelling; if there is an error, copy it and add *sic* in brackets. Enclose within double quotation marks all that you copy. See card A.

A

A

 "Later I realized that these images are also
found in primitive art. Mitchell explains that
visual representation is 'not radically
distinct from language,' and Elizabeth Abel
contends that the underlying concepts of myth
and art are similar in that both express a
'common inner source whose subject matter
changes but whose nature is the same.' "

A

When there are double quotation marks within the passage, they will
become single marks within your double ones. See card I if you think
you might use the quotes from Mitchell and Abel in your final paper.

B. Direct quotation of all or part of a passage with allowable changes:

   1. Ellipsis (the omission of a word or passage indicated by three periods
   with a space before and after and between each period). See card B.

B1

A

 "But gradually I realized that . . . those
marvelous tales were metaphorical expressions
of essential aspects of the human condition. "

B1

When any part of the quoted material depends for its meaning on a
word or passage that you have not included, either omit that item by
using ellipsis marks or else add inside of brackets an explanation of

the phrase, so that later you will know the reference and you will be aware that it is not part of the quoted section of the original text. See card B2.

2. Brackets (used to enclose material you add within the quotation or to indicate a change in the form of some word). See card B2.

B2

A

 "But gradually I realized that on another level [other than being fascinated by the narratives and sense of magic] those marvelous tales were metaphorical expressions of essential aspects of the human condition.'"

B2

The allusion to levels appeared in an earlier passage and needs to be inserted here if you are concerned with the various levels on which mythology is being considered.

3. Certain limited changes without brackets:

   a. Capitals may be made lowercase (or vice versa) if such a change will enable you to use the quotation as part of your own sentence. Lowercase letters may be capitalized if you want to begin a sentence in the middle of a sentence from your source. See card B3.

B3

A

 "When man attempts to explain the unknown, he is likely to depend on imagery from what he does know or on archetypal images which come out of his own inner experiences."

B3

In the original, *when* was not capitalized. Remember, von Franz must be given credit in a footnote to indicate that Markman was quoting this passage from her.

b. A final (or internal) punctuation mark within a quoted passage may be altered or omitted for the same reason. Or you may add a period if you terminate a quotation before the end of the sentence. See card B4.

B4

```
┌─────────────────────────────────────────────────────────┐
│  A                                                        │
├─────────────────────────────────────────────────────────┤
│ (iv)    "Each social group had obviously developed a      │
│         mythology by which it could understand the        │
│         basic experiences of its existence."              │
│                                                           │
└─────────────────────────────────────────────────────────┘
```

B4

In the original there was a comma after *existence*. An ellipsis is not needed here to show that sentence continues. Nothing from the text is omitted here nor is there any change in the context of the quoted passage.

c. Tense may be altered to make the material fit the context of your own paper. See card B5.

B5

```
┌─────────────────────────────────────────────────────────┐
│  A                                                        │
├─────────────────────────────────────────────────────────┤
│ (iv)    Markman agreed with von Franz that "when man      │
│         attempted to explain the unknown, he was likely   │
│         to depend on imagery from what he knew or on      │
│         archetypal images which came out of his own       │
│         inner experiences."                               │
│                                                           │
└─────────────────────────────────────────────────────────┘
```

B5

In the original *attempted* was present tense; *was* was present tense; *knew* was *does know* and *came* was present tense.

d. Italics in the original will be indicated by underlining. If, for emphasis, you want to italicize words not italicized in the original, so indicate after the quotation by parentheses in which you say (Italics mine). See card B6.

B6

```
┌─────────────────────────────────────────────────────┐
│                                                       │
│   A                                                   │
│  ─────────────────────────────────────────────────   │
│  (iv)   Markman identifies three stages of interest in│
│         mythology: she was fascinated at first by "the│
│         dramatic action of the narratives and the aura│
│         of magic," later by the "metaphorical         │
│         expression," and finally by the function and  │
│         methodology of mythology and art which have   │
│         many "common denominators." The world they    │
│         depict "may not be literally true," but both  │
│         verbal and visual forms do capture the        │
│         "essential truth" of the human condition.     │
│         (Italics mine).                                │
│                                                       │
└─────────────────────────────────────────────────────┘
```

B6

In the original the five quoted phrases were in different sentences and not necessarily in this order.

NOTE: These five short quoted passages would be documented in a single footnote.

C. Précis. This is a careful rewrite in your own words, usually about one-third the length of the original. In writing a précis, you are actually composing part of your paper. It is important to maintain the style, the point of view, and the tone of the original without using exact words or phrases from your source. See card C.

C

A	
(iv)	Markman was fascinated by the stories and magic of mythology. Later she realized they were metaphors by which life's mysteries were described and understood. Daily experiences and primordial images in man's psyche provided the sources of the imagery for these myths which, although not scientifically true, show valid insight into some basic areas of the human condition. Von Franz, Mitchell, and Abel are convinced that the visual arts share this function and manifest similar imagery. A comparative study of visual and verbal expression in primitive society would be instructive. (P)

C

A capital P in parentheses will remind you later that the words are your own; you would then footnote the idea but would not put quotation marks around it. Do the same for paraphrases.

D. Summary. This kind of note states in your own words and/or condenses the basic ideas of a long passage, chapter, or even whole book. See card D.

D

A	
(iv)	Verbal and visual expression serve similar functions with comparable imagery by which primitive societies have conceptualized their basic life experiences.

E. Outline. This kind of note reduces to organized form the basic information in a paragraph, page, or chapter. See card E.

E

A

 Myth and art are the media by which societies
express basic beliefs.
Through myth their beliefs are expressed in
verbal metaphor. Through art their beliefs are
expressed in visual metaphor.
Ultimately the medium and the imagery are
comparable.

F. Paraphrase. Use this with caution, for it is easy to be careless and end up being a plagiarist. You will avoid this danger if you read the passage well, close the book, and then write your paraphrase from memory. The paraphrase (see card F) is good to use

1. when you need to simplify some pedantic or esoteric passage;

2. when you rephrase or clarify another's definition or explanation;

3. when you put the lines of a poem into your own words.

F

A

 Markman states that the narratives and the
magical aura of mythology are fascinating. In
addition, one can read myths as a metaphoric
expression of some important beliefs about
life; they help a society to understand the
mysteries of birth, death, and the relationship
of man and nature. Even though these stories are
not scientifically true, they do tell some
basic truths about the human condition. Von

> Franz says that the imagery comes from the
> experience of everyday life or from the
> primordial images of man's psyche. Markman
> found that Mitchell and Abel documented her
> observation that primitive art also serves this
> function and utilizes the same kinds of
> imagery. She thinks a comparable study of the
> verbal and visual arts of primitive societies
> would be valuable. (P)

NOTE: Indicate the beginning of any paraphrase by informally mentioning the author and/or title, and be sure to note when other authors need to be given credit for an idea, as with Von Franz, Mitchell, and Abel above.

G. Combination note. While you are making your notes, you will occasionally find it advisable to weave a quotation into a sentence of your own to remind you of how you intended to use the material or to enable you to use the card intact in your rough draft. The only danger lies in possible carelessness: be sure to make clear (even exaggerated) quotation marks around the quoted part of the sentence to distinguish it from your own words. See card G.

G

A

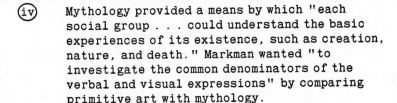

(iv)   Mythology provided a means by which "each
social group . . . could understand the basic
experiences of its existence, such as creation,
nature, and death." Markman wanted "to
investigate the common denominators of the
verbal and visual expressions" by comparing
primitive art with mythology.

H. Quotation taken from a footnote. It is important to indicate the source quoted in the footnote of the material you are reading; then any error in the quotation or publication data will be that author's, not yours. His or her source will not be included in your own bibliography unless you have also used it as one of your own sources. See card H.

H

A

   Markman states that Marie–Louise von Franz, Patterns of Creativity Mirrored in Creation Myths (Zürich: Spring Publications, 1978), p. 5, "based her conclusions [regarding the sources of imagery] on the images she has found on maps of antiquity."

I. Quotation of a quote. Use this rarely. If a quotation is valuable enough to quote, you should try to see the original from which the quote was taken. However, since some material used by other writers might be difficult for you to obtain, this kind of note might be necessary. The source quoted by the author you read will not be included in your bibliography unless you have actually used it as one of your own sources. See card I.

I

A

   "The underlying concepts of myth and art are similar in that both express a 'common inner source whose subject matter changes but whose nature is the same.' "

NOTE: If you used this sentence in your paper, your footnote would cite Markman as your source, not Abel. The identification at the top of the card already indicates that Markman is your source, but you need to note that she was quoting Abel. Then add bibliographical information about Abel's article; you may be able to locate and use it yourself.

J. Critical. You may wish to make an evaluation of the material you are reading or to write down your own ideas about it. This kind of note reminds you of judgments made during your reading. See card J.

A
Markman does not indicate clearly what the focus of the comparative study will be.

K. Synopsis or condensation. This is a summary of narrative material (i.e., a motion picture, a novel, a play, a narrative poem, etc.). No illustration card is given.

NOTE: Every completed notecard (see STEPS 6 and 7) should have six items on it:

1. source symbol

2. page number in a circle

3. the note itself

4. quotation marks around verbatim quotes OR the letter *P* to indicate your personal wording or paraphrase

5. the label (slug) or an outline symbol

6. on the back, information about where you discovered that this source exists AND a note to yourself about how or why you plan to use it.
    (If your instructor prefers, put this information on the back of the bibliography card instead.)

PUNCTUATION WITH QUOTATION MARKS—Remember these rules:

All commas and periods go *inside* the closing quotation marks.
All other punctuation goes inside *only* when it is a part of the quoted matter.
All semicolons go outside the closing marks.

STEP

LABEL NOTECARDS
AND REVISE
WORKING OUTLINE

After you have taken about half of your notes, you will observe that they can be categorized under several general headings. Often these headings coincide with the various units of your preliminary outline; on the other hand, they often suggest topics that need to be added to your outline. Remember, as you read, that you will not only be revising your preliminary outline but also reevaluating and reformulating your thesis statement in the light of your increased knowledge and accumulated information.

The items of your preliminary outline will provide the labels or slugs which you will write in pencil on the top lines of your notecards; pencil is better than ink here because you may want to change your label if you find later that a particular note could be used better under another heading. Some material cannot be categorized easily; leaves these notecards to be labeled later. Some notes will be particularly good as part of an introduction or a conclusion; use "intro." or "concl." as the slugs for these. Some notes will obviously not belong at all; mark these with an X and put them aside for the time being.

As you come closer to finishing your research, you will find that your notecards fall into four or five general categories, and these might turn out to be quite different from your original points for the temporary outline. You should now study your notecards and group them under general categories. Simply separate your cards into stacks, according to the ideas on them. This may take considerable time, but it is time well spent for in this way you will determine the organization of your entire paper.

If, for example, you were writing a paper to compare the visual and verbal metaphors by which various cultures have attempted to understand the basic phenomena of life, you might see that your cards can easily be divided into the basic areas of life that are most frequently the concern of both mythology and art. These might include the expression of the process of creation, the relationship of the individual (microcosm) to the universal (macrocosm), the conception of death and an afterlife, and so forth. These classifications could then become the Roman numerals for your outline. Then you would further divide your cards into several subpoint labels, and one notecard might be labeled thus:

R   God related to life/death–also water

(27)   In many myths "Death is presented as a figure opposite, but <u>complementary</u> to, the Creator as source of life." Sometimes a twin who becomes God of the underworld.

(28)   Water is also important to creation and yet is often the means of destruction of the world.

NOTE: This card would go with III A 1 on the outline for the paper, page 88.

If, on the other hand, you were doing your research on the subject of smog control, you might find that your notecards will fall into such categories as causes of the smog problem, manifestations of the smog problem, effects of smog on various aspects of the environment, solutions to the problem of smog control. These general classifications would then supply the Roman numerals for your outline.

You may find other possibilities for different classifications by studying the following as they might relate to your subject:

problem—cause—effect—solution
social causes—political causes—economic causes—psychological causes
the various effects (or solutions or manifestations) of some problem
different kinds of irony or values or attitudes
different (or similar) characteristics of something or someone
different ways of evaluating your topic
different advantages (or disadvantages) of a particular method, machine, approach, or process

Comparing and contrasting is a particularly instructive and creative way of organizing a documented paper. It enables the student to come to valuable conclusions by "measuring" one idea or area in terms of another. There are, however, three basic considerations to keep in mind:

1. Be sure before you begin that the two areas to be compared and contrasted have just enough in common to make them comparable without being ridiculously obvious or impossibly unrelated.

2. Be sure to qualify your points by telling to what extent and how one area is different from the other, thus avoiding the risk of overstating your case to the point of losing its credibility.

3. Be sure to compare and contrast the two areas *point by point* rather than discussing *all* of one area and then *all* of the other, thereby forcing your readers to determine the similarities and differences for themselves.

After you have found a way to divide your notecards into separate larger classifications, mark with a Roman numeral I all the cards in the classification you think you will discuss first in your paper; use a II for those you will discuss in the second part, and so on. Then take all the ones you have marked with numeral I and, considering them as material for a separate essay, determine into what categories you can further divide those ideas. For example, you might find that the pile of cards marked I, because they all deal with the causes of the smog problem (#2 in the list above), contain some that deal with problems related to industry, others deal with problems related to transportation, others with problems related to private homes. These would be divided into IA, IB, and IC. Then you would consider each of these sections separately. You might decide that those cards marked IA or IB do not need further division, but that those marked IC need to be divided into such categories as road transportation and air transportation, and you would mark the cards appropriately IC 1 and IC 2.

Remember in your outlining that you can never have a I without at least a II, nor an A without at least a B, nor a 1 without at least a 2, since logically nothing can be divided into fewer than two parts (not even apples). And your outline actually represents a division of ideas for the purpose of analyzing a subject in an organized fashion. At first, then, your notecards might have a label or slug like the example above; but once your outline is really set, you can save time by simply using the outline number instead.

Now you are ready to write the outline in its final form, taking care to word the items so that all Roman numerals (subdivisions of your thesis) are worded to be parallel in logic and in grammar; all the letter entries (A, B, C) are stated as parallel subdivisions of the Roman numeral under which they appear; and all the numbered entries (1, 2, 3) are logically and grammatically parallel subdivisions of the statement made in the letter under which they appear.

Before you can decide that you have finished your notetaking, you should examine your notecards to determine if you have adequate material for all the areas that are important to your thesis or a particular part of its proof. This evaluation will direct any subsequent notetaking to those specific topics for which you need more information, and you will then take only those notes which you know you will use. If you do take more notes on some new material that necessitates the inclusion of a new point, be sure to change your outline to include it.

STEP

WRITE THE FIRST DRAFT

Although you will never have the feeling that you have finished your notetaking to your satisfaction and you will never lose the feeling that you could do a much better job if you could examine "just one more source," the time for writing the first draft inevitably comes.

1. Check your thesis; be sure that it states as specifically as possible in a simple declarative sentence exactly what the material you have gathered adds up to.

2. Check your outline; be sure that each subtopic is directly relevant to the more general topic above it and, finally, that each major topic is directly relevant to the thesis. Make each item parallel to every other item both logically and grammatically. (That is, in a sentence outline, which is definitely preferable to a topic outline, be sure that each item is stated in a full sentence; in a topic outline, be sure that all items are stated in parallel parts of speech which are also parallel logically.) Check to see that no item overlaps another. Remember that no item can be divided into just one part: every I must have a II, every A must have a B, every 1 must have a 2, and so forth. Check to see that you have arranged the items of your outline in logical order: order of space or time, order of importance, order of complexity, and so forth. REMEMBER: Just as it is

better and more advantageous to detect the faults in a floor plan for a house on the blueprint than it is to find them in the finished building, so it is easier and more advantageous to find the errors of your logic and organization in your outline than it is to find them in your finished paper.

3. Your outline should now be ready for you to write in its final form if you have followed the instructions in STEP 6. If you have some notecards you cannot use (there are inevitably a few), do not destroy them; put them away, for you may be able to use them in writing some other paper in the future.

4. Do not begin by writing your introduction. Wait to write that when your paper is completed and you can see what you are introducing. Start now by putting on paper as quickly as possible the overall information you wish to convey about your major points and their subdivisions. Save the fun of polishing your style till later; first you must capture your ideas on paper so you can think about them.

    Develop your first point first. Arrange the notecards for your first Roman numeral to correspond with the order in that part of your outline and plunge right in as if you were writing a short essay with Roman numeral I as your thesis.

5. Write on one side of the paper only and skip a line between each line of your writing so that you can cross out poor or awkward phrases and add better wording without unnecessary recopying later when you revise. If you type your draft, triple space for the same reason.

6. If you use a direct quote in your paper, simply staple or clip the notecard on which it is written to the place where it belongs in your text. This will save time and avoid the possibility of inaccuracy as a result of recopying.

    It is very important to learn how to "weave" quoted or paraphrased material so that it becomes a part of your own text. Try not to use the colon to introduce any quotation unless it is long enough to block (i.e., one over three lines in length); otherwise, weave quotations into your own sentences so that a person hearing the paper read aloud would be unable to tell where a quote actually begins or ends. Make all quoted material sound like an integral part of your whole work; this means you must pay attention to point of view and tense. Not only does integrating the source material into your text add to the general unity and fluency of your writing, it also serves the even more important purpose of indicating the relevance of that source material to the content of your paper. In other words, before using a quoted or paraphrased passage, think of why you are using it or of what purpose it serves in your paragraph; then weave it into your text by indicating some relevance which you clarify in your own wording. It will then be valuable to your proof of thesis and its implications will be clear to your reader.

For example, in the following sentence from a discussion of Gerhart Hauptmann's play *The Weavers,* there is no doubt about the significance of the quotation used:

> The formula for success, which according to Master Wiegand is "cunning, quickness, and ruthless determination" [p. 30], had to be exposed and challenged.

Poorly used, the quotation might be inserted without any indication of relevance to the purpose of the paper, which (as here) might be a study of the values questioned in the play. An example of the same quotation, ineptly used, might read thus:

> Master Wiegand said: "Cunning, quickness, and ruthless determination are necessary" [p. 30].

Your reader would naturally wonder, "Necessary for what?" You might profit at this point by studying the sample paper on pages 86 to 99, which illustrates a variety of ways to incorporate quotations into your text. Note the punctuation also.

NOTE: The physical presence of the notecards on the first draft will do more than save you time and eliminate the possibility of inaccurate copying; it will also

   a. help you see if you are merely "stringing quotes" without enough of your own wording;

   b. keep you from using and footnoting the same information or the same quoted passage twice;

   c. help you check the way you introduce each quoted passage or phrase.

7. Even before you finish the first writing (rough draft), you may want to rearrange some material already written. If so, see the first two paragraphs under STEP 8; the directions there will facilitate your work if you decide to insert or change material as you write.

8. When you have taken information from a notecard, whether it is a directly quoted passage or not, stop where the passage ends and draw

in the cut-off lines across your page. Be sure to do this at the exact point where the material

AA, ⑦

calls for a footnote. Leave enough space so that you can fill in your full footnote later; right now, while your notecard is in your hand, simply put in the bibliography card identification letter (like AA above) and the page number (like ⑦ above) from which the information came. It is helpful to write footnote information in a different color of ink. It is essential to copy this information exactly; it is the only way that you can be assured that your documentation is accurate.

Put a check in the corner of the notecard that you have used so that you will be sure not to use the same information again. If your cut-off lines come in the middle of the sentence, continue after the cut-off lines as if they were not there.

9. Repeat this process to develop each of your Roman numerals, considering each as a separate essay for the time being. Just as you could not expect to write five essays in one day, so you cannot hope to develop more than one section of a long paper at a time.

10. Remember to revise your outline if you make any changes as you write your first draft. By the time you complete your first draft, your outline will be the blueprint of your actual paper.

11. Be sure to number the pages of your first draft; if you add pages to be inserted between pages already numbered, simply number the inserted pages also; for example, if they come after page 8, number the inserted pages 8A, 8B, and so on, but remember to renumber the inserted pages (and all subsequent pages) before typing your final copy.

STEP

REVISE THE TEXT; WRITE INTRODUCTION AND CONCLUSION

The best way to revise your work is to read your paper aloud after a waiting period. Avoid the necessity of recopying your work by using scissors to cut out material which belongs elsewhere. Be sure to cut out any footnote that belongs with a passage you are moving. Simply tape the whole insert where it belongs; you may need to cut that page in order to insert the interpolated material.

The advantage of keeping the footnote within cut-off lines immediately below the material it documents and the advantage of not numbering the footnotes until the paper is ready for typing are obvious here. You are free to move material around without recopying, without the chance of inaccurate documentation, and without having to renumber all of the succeeding footnotes. Your draft is supposed to look quite worked over, crossed out, and rearranged as a result of your revision.

1. Check to see that you have followed the basic rules for good English sentence structure and style.

2. Check to see that you have followed the principles of rhetoric in your sentence structure, paragraph development, and diction.

3. Check to see that you have smooth transitions (connections) from sentence to sentence, paragraph to paragraph, and section to section.

Check particularly to see that the quoted material is integrated into the text so that, together with your writing, it presents a unified piece of work. Check also the punctuation before and after the quoted material used as part of your own sentence; a good test is to ask yourself whether you would use a comma, a colon, or other punctuation if there were no quotation marks within that sentence. (See Card G, page 53.) When you hear a well-prepared lecture, you are not aware that the lecturer has gathered material from many different sources, part of which he or she is quoting directly and some of which is being paraphrased. You should give the same impression to your reader. Often the addition of a few connecting words will result in smooth transitions.

4. Check to see that your finished paper sounds logically developed and that everything that you have included in your paper presents relevant, logical proof of your thesis.

5. Check to see that you have avoided the repetition of facts or ideas. A "padded" paper is boring and meaningless.

WRITE THE INTRODUCTION

Now that you know exactly what you are about to introduce, you can write an introductory section to your paper. You can use your introduction to do the following:

1. point out the timeliness or value of your research;

2. define an abstract or special term used in your thesis;

3. explain why you have taken this particular aspect of your topic;

4. inform your reader of the various aspects of your topic other than the one you have chosen;

5. give a pertinent anecdote which provides a direct means of leading into your topic;

6. summarize how you have approached your topic.

Whatever your approach, your introduction should be relevant; it should gain the immediate attention of your reader; and it should clarify your thesis in some way.

WRITE THE CONCLUSION

The conclusion of the research paper is the most valuable single part of it. All the material you have gathered means nothing to your reader until you present the conclusion you have reached as a result of your research. Restate your thesis and show what the material you have presented adds up to. Analyze and evaluate your main points for you reader; also consider the ramifications and general implications of them to your conclusion. Actually, the conclusion is the only "original" contribution you offer in your paper. It manifests the value of your research as well as your understanding of the material which you have presented.

STEP

FILL IN FOOTNOTES ON DRAFT

Before you put your paper into its final copy form, you need to fill in the footnotes within the cut-off lines and write them as they will appear in your final paper. Normally, every paragraph except those which develop your own completely original ideas will have at least one footnote.

WHAT TO FOOTNOTE

1. All important statements of fact and all opinions, whether directly quoted or paraphrased, and all paraphrases of those facts which are not common knowledge should be documented by a footnote reference to the exact page in the source where you found your information. If you are not quoting printed matter, your footnote should tell the reader where and how you found out the particular material you need to document.

2. Definitions that would interrupt the text but might be helpful to the reader should be in a footnote. See footnote 29 of the sample paper (pages 86-99).

3. Material that would detract from the focus of your paper but which would supply valuable and enriching information to the reader should be in a

footnote, not in the text of your paper. This material may be in your own words or in words you quote from an authority. Also, the footnote may simply refer the reader to another source or sources where a fuller discussion may be found. See footnotes 9, 10, 28, 40, and 44 of the sample paper.

4. Cross-references may be suggested in a footnote. Often you want to show the existence of contradictory information or to refer your reader to additional sources. See footnotes 39 and 40 of the sample paper.

5. Cross-references to other parts of your own paper may be made in footnotes. See footnotes 31 and 34 of the sample paper.

WHAT NOT TO FOOTNOTE

1. Well-known, generally accepted facts need not be footnoted unless you want to document someone's questioning of those facts.

2. Any material which comes from commonly recognized sources or quotations need not be footnoted; you may say that all men are created equal or that all the world's a stage or that the heavens declare the glory of God without referring in context or footnote to the Declaration of Independence, to Shakespeare, or to the Bible, respectively.

HOW TO COMPLETE FOOTNOTES WITHIN CUT-OFF LINES

After the last revision, go through the text of your rough draft once more and number the items to be footnoted. Put the number after the last word before the cut-off lines and above the line of writing. If you are documenting a direct quote, put the number after the closing quotation mark. Put the same number after the abbreviated symbol for the source already within the cut-off lines. Your footnote number will then be indented as it must be when you put the paper into final form. Number consecutively throughout your paper.

You will now use the completed bibliography card to complete your footnote. For every first-entry footnote (the first time you document information from a source) you will give the complete bibliographical information *plus* the exact page number which you have already entered in the cut-off lines. For all succeeding footnotes referring to that source, use the second-entry form.

Indent the first line of each footnote as for a paragraph and bring each succeeding line of the same footnote back to the margin.

PROCEDURE FOR WRITING FOOTNOTES

1. Take out the bibliography card indicated by the letter or symbol already entered in the cut-off lines.

2. Write your footnote as you would a sentence; do not separate into lines as you did on the bibliography card.

3. Write the number of the footnote in either of two ways, but be consistent:
   a. above the line as it must be in the text or
   b. on the same line as the footnote will be.

   For the former, use no period after the number; for the latter, be sure to use a period and two spaces before beginning your footnote. Check to see that the number in the text matches the number given for the footnote. Remember that footnotes are numbered consecutively throughout the paper; there will be only one footnote numbered 1 in any short paper (fewer than fifty typewritten pages) or for each chapter in a long paper.

4. Indent the footnote number and first line as for a paragraph; bring the second and each succeeding line of the same note back to the margin of the text.

5. Fill in all information from the bibliography card exactly as it is written with these exceptions:
   a. write the author's name in regular order (not reversed) followed by a comma, not a period;
   b. omit the period after the name of a book; put a comma instead of a period after the name of an article;
   c. enclose within parentheses the publication facts for a book (city, publisher, date), omitting the period after the date; put a comma after the parentheses.

6. Copy exactly the page number already after the symbol at the beginning of the cut-off lines; unless a volume number is given, put the abbreviation for *page* before the page number. If a pamphlet or booklet

has no page number, supply a page number in brackets or write the words *no page* after the comma.

7. Put a period at the end of the footnote.

8. Check the page number you had entered in the cut-off lines after the symbol for the source to be sure it matches the page number in the footnote; cross out both symbol and page number, leaving only the completed footnote form within the cut-off lines.

9. Before you put your bibliography card away, put a check mark by the identifying letter or symbol on it (the one you used on notecards) to show that you have used this source once for a first-entry footnote.

10. All future references to this source or to any other source already documented in full will be in second-entry footnote form.

HOW TO WRITE FOOTNOTES ON THE FINAL COPY

Decide where you are going to put your footnotes; there are three acceptable places:

1. at the bottom of the same page on which the footnote number occurs in the text. For this place, triple space after the last line of text and then make a line by striking the underline key fifteen times; then double space before writing the footnote number. Before writing the footnote itself, give the typewriter carriage half a turn downward. Remember to indent the first line of each footnote five spaces as if for a paragraph; bring the rest of the footnote back to the margin. Single space each entry; double space between each footnote entry.

2. on a separate page at the end of a short paper or at the end of each chapter for a long paper. On this page, center and type the title in capitals (FOOTNOTES) with no underlining; put the page number in the center at the bottom of the page. If there is more than one page, put no heading or title on the next page but continue to number in the upper right-hand corner to match the pagination on other pages.

3. in the text itself. It is becoming increasingly popular for instructors to suggest that relatively short papers be documented within the text itself in order to avoid numerous footnotes at the bottom of the page or at the end of the paper on a separate page. This in-text documentation is especially desirable when a student uses only one source or only a few sources about a given subject. To use in-text documentation, give the first-entry footnote in full at the bottom of the page as explained in paragraph 1 above or within the text itself as explained on page 81; then insert in brackets each succeeding footnote for any quote or paraphrase from that source, placing the brackets directly after it (see examples below). Generally, if the footnote contains a definition or explanation or if it is more than three-fourths of a line in length, you should use the regular footnote form at the bottom of the page or at the end of your paper.

EXAMPLES OF IN-TEXT DOCUMENTATION

If you were doing a critical analysis of a single text, such as Faulkner's *The Sound and the Fury,* you would give a formal first-entry footnote after your first reference to the book. You would add a sentence after that footnote and as a part of it, stating that all future references to this text are from the same edition. Then the second time you document from the book, your text would look like this:

Mrs. Compson looks upon Benjy as "a judgment" [p. 25], and she changes his name, not wanting an idiot child to bear the name of her brother because she is "too proud" [p. 89].

NOTE: The punctuation comes after the bracket closes.

If you are using two texts by the same author, you would give the first-entry footnotes in full for each book; for all later quotations you would give the name of the work in brackets so that your reader would know to which of the two sources your documentation refers. For example: [*The Sound and the Fury,* p. 62] or [*Light in August,* p. 104].

If you are using several texts all by different authors, you would give the first-entry footnotes in full as in both cases above and then put the author's name and the page in brackets after the reference, thus:

[Miller, p. 240] or [Shaw, p. 69].

NOTE: Once you have decided where you are going to put your footnotes, copy the footnote exactly as you have written it within the cut-off lines. Remember to single space the lines within each footnote entry and to double space between entries.

FOOTNOTE FORMS

The following examples show the footnote form for each of the bibliography cards and entries used in STEP 4, pages 19 to 36.

FORMS FOR FIRST-ENTRY FOOTNOTES
From a Source with Its Own Title

NOTE: When typing your own footnotes remember that you will underline all items that appear in *italics.*

Some writers do not include in footnotes all of the publication data if a bibliography is given at the end of the paper; however, many colleges do require the following full form as well as a bibliography.

1. the basic form

[1] Joseph Campbell, *Myths to Live By* (New York: The Viking Press, 1972), p. 28.

2. no author

[2] *Máscaras Mexicanas: de la Colección del Ing. Victor José Moya* (Mexico City: Dirección de Museos del Instituto Nacional de Antropología e Historia, 1974), pp. 97-99.

3. two authors

[3] C. A. Burland and Werner Forman, *Feathered Serpent and Smoking Mirror* (New York: G. P. Putnam's Sons, 1975), p. 36.

4. more than two authors

[4] José López Portillo and others, *Quetzalcoatl* (Mexico City: Secretaría de Asentamientos Humanos y Obras Públicas, 1977), p. 34.

5. corporate authorship

[5] Committee on College Teaching, *College Teaching as a Career* (Washington, D.C.: American Council on Education, 1958), p. 12.

6. an author and an editor

[6] William Wordsworth, *The Prelude or Growth of a Poet's Mind,* ed. Ernest de Selincourt (New York: Oxford University Press, 1947), pp. 73-74.

7. an author and a translator

[7] Mircea Eliade, *Images and Symbols,* trans. Philip Mairet (Kansas City, Missouri: Sheed Andrews and McMeel, 1961), p. 152.

8. an author, an editor, and a translator

[8] Pablo Neruda, *A New Decade (Poems: 1958-1967),* ed. Ben Belitt, trans. Ben Belitt and Alastair Reid (New York: Grove Press, 1969), p. 105.

9. an editor but no author

[9] W. J. T. Mitchell, ed., *The Language of Images* (Chicago: The University of Chicago Press, 1980), p. 41.

NOTE: This form would be used when referring to a section of an anthology other than one of the individually titled pieces as well as for any other book with an editor but no author; for a reference to an essay in this anthology, see example 29.

10. a compiler

[10] Curt Muser, comp., *Facts and Artifacts of Ancient Middle America* (New York: E. P. Dutton, 1978), p. 44.

11. one volume in a multivolume set when all volumes have the same title

[11] E. A. Wallis Budge, *The Gods of the Egyptians or Studies in Egyptian Mythology* (1904; rpt. New York: Dover Publications, 1969), II, 361.

NOTE: When both a volume number and a page number are given, neither the abbreviation *vol.* for volume nor *p.* for page is used.
This book is a modern reprint of an older edition; see example 16.

12. one volume in a multivolume set when each volume has a separate title

[12] John Russell, *The Dominion of the Dream,* vol. VII of *The Meanings of Modern Art* (New York: The Museum of Modern Art, 1975), p. 29.

13. a book in a series edited by one other than the author

[13] David Maclagen, *Creation Myths: Man's Introduction to the World,* in the *Art and Imagination* series, ed. Jill Purce (London: Thames and Hudson, 1977), pp. 112-115.

14. a book with a subtitle or secondary title

[14] Vincent F. Hopper, ed. and trans., *Chaucer's Canterbury Tales: An Interlinear Translation* (Woodbury, New York: Barron's, 1970), p. 17.

NOTE: Obviously Chaucer did not write a book with this title; therefore this entry is correct for this book. However, if you quoted the lines from Chaucer with the older spelling, your footnote would be thus:

[14] Geoffrey Chaucer, "The Pardoner's Tale," *Chaucer's Canterbury Tales: An Interlinear Translation,* ed. and trans. Vincent F. Hopper (Woodbury, New York: Barron's, 1970), p. 299.

15. an edition subsequent to the first edition

[15] Geoffrey Parrinder, *African Traditional Religion,* 3rd ed. (New York: Harper & Row, 1976), p. 137.

16. a modern reprint of an older edition

[16] Frances Toor, *Mexican Popular Arts* (1939; rpt. Detroit: Blaine Ethridge Books, 1973), p. 106.

17. a pamphlet, bulletin, or manual

[17] Marjorie M. Halpin, *Viewing Objects in Series: The Raven Rattle,* UBC Museum of Anthropology Note No. 6 (Vancouver: University of British Columbia Museum of Anthropology, 1978), p. [3].

NOTE: Brackets around the page number indicate that the pages in the pamphlet are not numbered and that the writer of the footnote has supplied the number.

18. a catalog of an exhibition

[18] Betty Ann Brown, curator, *Máscaras: Dance Masks of Mexico and Guatemala,* an exhibit at the Ewing Museum of Nations, Illinois State University, April 21-December 16, 1978 (Bloomington, Illinois: University Museums, Illinois State University, 1978), p. 27.

19. a government document

[19] U.S. Congressional Record, 80th Cong., 2nd Sess., 1948, XCII, Part 6, 5539.

20. a dictionary

[20] *Webster's New Collegiate Dictionary* (Springfield, Massachusetts: G. & C. Merriam Company, 1976).

NOTE: No page number is required since the dictionary is arranged alphabetically.

21. a record or tape

[21] Franz Liszt, *Late Piano Works,* Alfred Brendel, piano (Philips, 9500 775).

22. a film

[22] *Romeo and Juliet,* directed and produced by Franco Zeffirelli (Paramount Pictures, 1968).

23. a radio program

[23] *The Art of Hilde Gueden* (KUSC 91.5 FM, Los Angeles, 10:00 am July 1, 1981).

24. a television program

[24] *Hidden Places: Where History Lives,* pt. I (KCET, Channel 28, Los Angeles, 9:30 pm, August 7, 1981).

From Sources Contained in a Larger Work

25. the basic form

[25] Bart McDowell, "The Aztecs," *National Geographic,* December, 1980, p. 704.

26. a magazine article with no author

[26] "The Trajectories of Genius," *Time,* May 26, 1980, p. 79.

27. an untitled book review

[27] Herbert M. Cole, Review of *Two Thousand Years of Nigerian Art* by Ekpo Eyo, *African Arts,* February, 1979, p. 17.

NOTE: If this review had had a title, it would have been given in quotation marks after the name of the reviewer, Cole; the footnote would then continue as above.

28. a newspaper article or editorial

[28] Sylvie Drake, "Santa Fe: Artists in the Desert," *Los Angeles Times,* August 5, 1981, VI, 1.

NOTE: For an unsigned article, you would begin with the title of the article. VI, 1 indicates that the information to which you are referring is on page 1 of section VI. Note that when both a section (or volume) number and a page number are given, neither the abbreviation *sec.* for section (or *vol.* for volume) nor *p.* for page is used.

29. an essay (or other article) written by one person in an anthology edited by another

[29] Giulo Carlo Argan, "Ideology and Iconology," *The Language of Images,* ed. W. J. T. Mitchell (Chicago: The University of Chicago Press, 1980), p. 17.

30. an encyclopedia article

[30] Alan Dundes, "Myth: Myths of the Beginning and of the End," *Encyclopaedia Britannica* (1970), XV, 1136.

NOTE: As in example 28 above, both the abbreviations *vol.* and *p.* have been omitted.
For an unsigned article, you would begin with the title of the article. Remember that most articles are signed with initials only; you must look at the beginning of the first volume to find the author's full name.

31. an introduction or limited part of a book by one other than the author

[31] Peter T. Furst, "Foreword" to Donald Cordry, *Mexican Masks* (Austin, Texas: University of Texas Press, 1980), p. xii.

32. author of part of a book in a series edited by others

[32] Herbert Mason, "Myth as an 'Ambush of Reality,' " *Myth, Symbol, and Reality,* ed. Alan M. Olson, vol. I of the Boston University Studies in Philosophy and Religion, ed. Leroy S. Rouner (Notre Dame, Indiana: University of Notre Dame Press, 1980), p. 18.

33. a reprint with critical comment by the editor

[33] Andrew Wright, "Afterword" in Joyce Cary, *The Horse's Mouth* (1944; rpt. New York: Perennial Library—Harper & Row, 1965), p. 349.

34. a casebook (a text for controlled research)

[34] David Stevenson, "J. D. Salinger: The Mirror of Crisis," *The Nation,* March 9, 1957, p. 215; rpt. *If You Really Want to Know: A Catcher Casebook,* ed. Malcolm M. Marsden (Chicago: Scott, Foresman, 1963), p. 22.

NOTE: There are two ways to use a casebook: as an anthology of essays about a particular subject or as a library containing essays which you will read and document as if you were reading the original. For the latter use, the original pagination appears in the casebook with slash marks wherever a page change occurred in the original. Check with your instructor about how to use the casebook, but it would never be wrong to use the form above.

From Other Types of Sources

35. an interview

[35] Roberta H. Markman, Professor of Comparative Literature, California State University, Long Beach, personal interview on Mexican masks, Long Beach, California, April 16, 1980.

NOTE: Unless the person interviewed is well known, you should indicate through the use of the person's title why he or she is an authority on the subject of the interview.

36. an unpublished lecture

[36] Peter T. Markman, Professor of English, Fullerton College, class lecture on Carlos Fuentes, *The Death of Artemio Cruz,* Fullerton College, Fullerton, California, May 3, 1981.

37. a published lecture

[37] Kurt Vonnegut Jr., "Address to Graduating Class at Bennington College, 1970," *Wampeters, Foma and Granfalloons (Opinions)* (New York: Dell, 1976), p. 163.

38. mimeographed material

[38] Betty Ann Brown, "Fiestas de Oaxaca," 1977 (mimeographed), p. 3.

39. an unpublished thesis or dissertation

[39] Roberta H. Markman, "Mann's Joseph: From Dreamer to Artist," unpublished Ph.D. dissertation, Dept. of Comparative Literature, Occidental College, Los Angeles, 1969, p. 308.

40. a letter

[40] Unpublished letter from Ernest Hemingway to Roberta Hoffman, August 12, 1957.

41. The Bible or any well-known literary work which can be identified by book or scene plus lines or by chapter and verse

[41] I Corinthians 13:12, The Bible, Revised Standard Version.

NOTE: The names of sacred scripture are neither underlined nor put in quotation marks. The translation of the Bible is assumed to be the King James Version unless another is named, as in the example above.

[41] John Milton, *Paradise Lost,* bk. I, ll. 13-14.

NOTE: The particular edition you used is not needed unless the work is a translation.
The name of a novel, play, or long poem would be underlined even if it is part of an anthology.

42. an abridgment

[42] *Style Manual* (abridged), rev. ed. (Washington, D.C.: Government Printing Office, 1959), p. 19.

43. record jacket information

[43] *The Bitter and the Sweet,* Pete Seeger (Columbia Records, CS 8716, 1962), jacket notes.

44. a pamphlet included with a record

[44] Richard Kostelanetz and Editors of Time-Life Records, "A Listener's Guide to the Recordings," *The Music of Today* in *The Story of Great Music* series (Time-Life Records, STL 145), p. 3.

45. a lecture on a record or tape

[45] Thomas Scherman, narrator and conductor, "Musical Program Notes," Beethoven's *Symphony No. 5 in C Minor, Op. 67,* Sir Adrian Boult conducting The Philharmonic Promenade Orchestra of London (Vanguard, MARS 3005).

ABBREVIATED FORMS FOR SECOND-ENTRY FOOTNOTES

When you take out a bibliography card and see the check which indicates that you already have a first-entry footnote for that source, use the appropriate second-entry form for that and all subsequent footnotes referring to that source. The abbreviated, second-entry forms for footnotes have traditionally been given in Latin terms, but current usage seems to indicate the eventual elimination of all Latin from footnotes.

Some scholars have already eliminated all Latin terms except *ibid. Vide* has already been replaced by *see,* which is shorter; *op. cit.* and *loc. cit.* are considered obsolete and are no longer required in many schools. However, since they are still frequently found in older reference materials, you need to know what they signify. You will find an explanation below.

1. for a footnote which is identical in all respects to the last footnote referring to any source:

There may be intervening footnotes (giving a definition, an explanation, or a cross-reference) between ibid. and the source to which it refers so long as no other source is mentioned in them.

[1] Ibid.

The previous source need not be mentioned on the same page as ibid.

Although ibid. may be the first footnote to appear on a page, it obviously could never be the first footnote of a paper.

2. for a footnote identical in all respects except page number to the last footnote referring to any source (see note above):

With or without a page number, ibid. is no longer used by many scholars; the last

[2] Ibid., p. 16.

name of the author and the page

number are often used instead. See the
footnotes on pages 93-96 listed after the
sample paper.

3. **for a footnote referring to a source after which another source
intervenes (there are two acceptable forms):**

[3] Campbell, p. 3.   This form will adequately identify any
source already cited in full except when
there are two sources by the same author
or two authors with the same last name.
See 4 and 5 below.

[3] Campbell, op. cit., p. 3. Although you may not be required to use
this form, you will still find it in some
older writings and will need to know
what it means.

4. **for a footnote referring to a source if you have used two or more
sources by the same author:**

[4] Campbell, *Myths to Live By*, p. 3.

[4] Campbell, "*Myths . . . ,*" To distinguish which of his works you are
p. 3.   quoting, give the author's last name, the
full title of the source or a shortened form
of it, and the page number.

5. **for a footnote to distinguish between two or more authors with the
same last name:**

[5] Joseph Campbell, p. 3. This would be enough if you have
previously cited only one work by this
author.

[5] Joseph Campbell, *Myths to Live By*, p. 3.

            If you have previously cited two or more
sources by this author, give also the title
or a shortened form of it to show which
source you are now citing.

6. for a footnote referring to a source without an author:

[6] "The Trajectories of Genius," p. 79.

[6] "The Trajectories . . . ," p. 79.

        A title may be shortened by using an ellipsis.

7. for an incomplete second-entry footnote:

[7] P. 65.   Use this form only if the author and source are already indicated in the text. Because it begins the footnote, P is capitalized.

[7] *Myths to Live By,* p. 3.   Use this form if you have named the author in the text and have also previously identified his work in a first-entry footnote.

NOTE: Although it is more helpful to your reader to see the full second-entry footnote, any information given in the text *may* correctly be omitted from the footnote. For example, if you name the author and/or his or her work in your text, you may omit that information from your footnote and supply only what is needed to identify your exact source accurately. Therefore the above forms are sometimes used for second-entry footnotes.

FORM FOR IN-TEXT DOCUMENTATION

When it is expedient to document within the text itself (e.g., when there will be only one or two references in a short paper), you must still give complete bibliographical information. This may be given in an informal way within your own sentence:

> On page 27 of his *Myths to Live By,* published in New York by The Viking Press in 1972, Joseph Campbell says that "the serpent shedding its skin, to be, as it were, born again, is likened in the Orient to the reincarnating spirit that assumes and throws off bodies as a man puts on and puts off clothes."

Or it may be given in this formal way or some variation of it:

> Joseph Campbell (*Myths to Live By* [New York: The Viking Press 1972], p. 44) believes that ritual serves "to give form to human life."

(See also page 71.)

STEP

PUT THE PAPER IN
FINAL FORM

THE ELEMENTS

1. Format

If possible, a research paper should be typewritten on regular (never thin) paper and double spaced except for blocked quotations, footnotes, and bibliography; otherwise, it should be written in blue or black ink as neatly and legibly as possible. Leave good margins on all four sides of the paper, allowing sufficient extra room on the left side for binding. The finished paper should be fastened and bound in a folder with the title, your name, the course, and the date on the outside.

2. Title Page

Include a title page on which you state the title of the paper, your name, the course (and section number, if any) for which the paper was written, the name of the institution (often considered optional), and the date the paper is submitted.

3. Preface

The dedication or the preface page, if there is one, is inserted after the title page; it is not numbered. The title of the page, DEDICATION or PREFACE, is centered and typed with capital letters.

4. Outline

The outline page serves as a table of contents, although it is not necessary to show page numbers for the short paper. The title of the page, OUTLINE, is centered and typed in capital letters. The page is numbered, and since the first page of your outline is a title page, the number is centered at the bottom of the page and is given in Roman numerals (lower case) because nothing is numbered in Arabic numerals until the first page of the text.

After the title, OUTLINE, skip two spaces and state the thesis sentence (after the word THESIS:). Follow that statement with the outline proper.

5. First Page of Text

The title of your paper is centered on the first (and no other) page of the text and typed in capital letters.

6. Footnotes

The footnotes will be written exactly as you have filled them in on the rough draft of your paper. For detailed information concerning footnote forms on the final copy, see STEP 9, the section entitled "How to write footnotes on the final copy," pages 70 to 81. All footnotes should be completed on the page where they begin.

NOTE: There may be a rare occasion when you need to continue a footnote onto the following page. If so, it will continue as a sentence (without interruption) and will go immediately after the line separating text from footnotes or onto the next (untitled) page if you are placing footnotes at the end of your paper.

7. Pagination

Every page which is a title page (i.e., the first page of the outline, of the footnotes, and of the bibliography; the dedication page; the preface; and so forth) is numbered at the bottom center of that title page. The number is written usually without punctuation. All other pages of the paper are numbered in the upper right-hand corner of the page; the number is written alone or followed by a period. The pages are numbered consecutively from the first page of the theme to the last page of the bibliography.

8. Quotations

Short quotations: Quoted short passages and/or sentences are woven into the text of your paragraph and should blend smoothly with your own style and the tense you are using. In the sample research paper on pages 86-99 you will see many examples of quotations (and paraphrases) woven into the text and made meaningful by the context in which they appear. Notice that before and after each quoted passage the punctuation is determined by what is needed to make the passage fit smoothly into the sentence. In other words, the test for punctuating before or after a quoted passage is this: Would you need a mark of punctuation at that point in your sentence if there were no quotation marks?

Longer (blocked) quotations: Sometimes, as in the footnotes numbered 3, 21, and 30 of the sample paper (see pp. 93 to 95), a quoted passage is too long to be woven into your own sentence; it is an entity in itself and must be set off from the paragraph in which it appears. In fact, any directly quoted material which is longer than three lines must be blocked and single-spaced.

To set off a blocked passage: Double space before the quote; indent seven spaces for each regular line. Indent twelve spaces if the quotation itself begins with a new paragraph and seven spaces for each succeeding, single-spaced line. Stop seven spaces before the right-hand margin begins. Single space each line of the quoted passage, and then double space before the text of your paper continues. If the quoted and blocked passage is longer than one paragraph, double space between paragraphs within the same blocked passage. Do not use quotation marks at the beginning or end since the single spacing is a substitute for them. However, you would use double or single quotation marks even in a blocked passage to enclose any material which is in double or single quotation marks in the source you are citing. In other words, a blocked quoted passage looks exactly as it did in the source you used.

Footnote number: The footnote number is put above the line and after the closing quotation mark or after the last word in a blocked passage.

9. Bibliography

The final bibliography is always the last section of a research paper. See STEP 4 for final bibliography forms.

10. Final Step

Proofread your paper carefully for typographical errors and use black ink to fill in brackets if needed.

A SAMPLE RESEARCH PAPER

NOTE: Since it is neither expedient nor necessary to reproduce an entire paper for the sake of illustrating the techniques explained in this manual, the pages that follow contain a full sentence outline and only that part of the paper which expands the thesis. (Normally, the first part of any research paper, the introduction, develops the thesis and clarifies the point of view from which the writer has limited his or her paper.) Also included is a bibliography listing only the sources used in this introductory section of the longer paper by Markman, from which this introductory section is taken. Normally, a short research paper such as this one would not have as many footnotes or as much quoted material; however, it is important for the student to see how a wide variety of material could be used and documented.

THE METAPHORIC VISION IN 'Y''H°IOG iNL ARI
by
Roberta H. Markman

Comparative Literature 452, Section 1
California State University, Long Beach
January 3, 1982

OUTLINE

Thesis: Humanity's attempt to understand the basic phenomena
of life is expressed metaphorically both verbally in
mythology and visually in art.

  I. The process of creation is expressed metaphorically in both mythology and art.

    A. Both mythology and art express the concept of
genesis through the metaphoric image of the
joining of opposites.

      1. Sometimes the primordial couple (the join-
ing of masculine and feminine) provides the
metaphor in both mythology and art.

      2. Sometimes the integration of light and dark
is the metaphoric image for the creative
process in both mythology and art.

      3. Sometimes the weaving of warp and woof
(vertical and horizontal) serves as the
imagery for creation.

    B. Both mythology and art express the concept of
creation through the metaphor of the sun's
pattern of dying and rising.

    C. Both mythology and art show "the beginning"
through the imagery of order emerging from
chaos.

    D. Both mythology and art express the creative
process as the splitting of the whole, or
single image, into two or more of its parts.

  II. Humanity's relationship to the universe is expressed metaphorically in both mythology and
art.

i

A. Both mythology and art describe various aspects of nature in their relationship to the
individual to show the complex relationship of
the individual to the universal.

B. Both mythology and art use the imagery of the
human being and God(s) to express and understand the relationship of the unique to the
general.

III. The conception of death and an afterlife are
metaphorically expressed in both mythology and
art in an attempt to come to terms with these
mysteries.

A. The phenomena of a symbolic death is expressed
metaphorically in both mythology and art.

1. The imagery of humanity's transcendent
temporal experience is expressed metaphorically in both mythology and art.

2. The imagery of the human being's return
from death, darkness or the underworld to a
new life is often the metaphor for the
experience of death and resurrection.

B. Physical death and a spiritual return, or
transcendence, is shown metaphorically in
both mythology and art.

THE METAPHORIC VISION IN MYTHOLOGY AND ART

As early as the second or third millennium B.C., with the epic of Gilgamesh and the later story of creation in Genesis, people have been challenged to "name" the animals and other elements of their world because "naming" in its truest sense signifies both an understanding of the basic nature of things and having dominion over them.[1] People seem always to have known that their successful existence as human beings depended on their understanding the basic phenomena of life and "knowing the world."[2]

Once they began to question the mysteries beyond measurable phenomena, primitive people faced the task of naming those aspects of life, such as creation and death, that remained outside the realms of intellect and logic. This quest has been a very difficult one for our scientific Western technocracy, but

> non-technical societies have maintained far more of an equilibrium. They have accepted the motivation to think and to know, but they have not afforded intellectuality the priority that it has in technical cultures.[3]

In fact, their challenge to know and to "name" the unknown provided not only the security that every society seeks but also the most powerful impetus for primitive art[4] because both mythology and art serve "to kindle into meaning aspects of their perception that would otherwise remain external to their minds."[5] As did King Arthur, the individual must begin this quest with the question that triggers the creative process and culminates in renewal.[6] Once the realm beyond the knowable is reached, says von Franz, one "projects an archetypal image"[7] by which, through mythology and art, insight regarding the fundamental areas of life is brought into reality.[8] Since myths and art "speak about the unknowable in terms of the known,"[9] they provide a means of transmitting an understanding of reality that results from the intensity of the involvement of humanity's confrontation with it.[10]

1

2

Because art and mythology have the crucial ability to communicate[11] and to "articulate . . . an inarticulate primary vision,"[12] they serve an important educational function in the community by expressing its beliefs and the meaning of its existence.[13] Pemberton illustrates this point in his discussion of the verses of the Odu by showing that myth and art, by expressing the world views and values of Yoruba culture, show the society how they can cope with problems, and Ifa verses explain the varying roles of human beings and of the powers that shape their lives as well as the powers by which they can improve them.[14] Because myths serve such functions as these, there seems to be no question among scholars that myth is absolutely essential to existence[15] or that "mere purposive rationality, unaided by such phenomena as art, religion, dream . . . is necessarily pathogenic and destructive of life."[16]

Both mythology and art do, in fact, create a kind of cosmic order out of what appears to be chaos,[17] and by so doing are clearly not the opposite of science[18] or less valuable than logic.[19] They too reveal something universally valid about the nature of reality.[20] Great myths and art are concerned with capturing the essence of their subjects, as Ray points out in her discussion of an Eskimo mask when she explains how the mask captured the essence, not of an individual animal

> but the vital force representing a chain or continuum of all the individual spirits of that genus which had lived, were living, or were to live.[21]

Its "truth" then, is not dependent on reproducing the details of a visual reality but, going beyond the object using a creative and interpretive approach, its nonrepresentative concern permits a "freedom from mere ideas"[22] and from the limitations of the " 'historic moment.' "[23]

Many scholars have compared the verbally expressed mythology and the visually expressed art of primitive societies by considering their methodologies as well as their functions and thematic concerns. Wittgenstein suggests that a verbal proposition is a picture that

3

represents a possible situation in logical space.[24] Human beings think in terms of images and, according to von Franz, "the only reality we can talk about . . . is the _image_ of reality in our field of consciousness,"[25] and it is with that realization that Jacques Waardenburg can say that a myth "can be called a 'moving symbolism.' "[26] Others have also investigated this relationship. Cassirer points out that "word magic is everywhere accompanied by picture magic,"[27] and Abel shows that both mythology and art express a "common inner source whose subject matter changes but whose nature is the same."[28]

Ultimately, however, there is no doubt that

> the relationship between word and image is, potentially, at once metonymic[29] and metaphoric: metonymic in that the two complete each other sequentially and as parts of a whole: metaphoric in that each translates into the other's medium. Ideally, image melts into speech, speech crystallizes the immediacy of the image.[30]

And it is primarily as metaphors that art and mythology are able to serve "as poetic expressions of . . . transcendental seeing."[31] By bringing together "_two_ _frames_ _of_ _reference_ of which the reader [or viewer] must be simultaneously aware"[32] both art and mythology can "bring truth into being"[33] and serve the essential functions that have been attributed to them.[34] By juxtaposing everyday experiences to the transcendent images of imagination, the mundane is transformed[35] into a revelation of the " 'extraordinary' aspects of ordinary reality."[36] As he wears a mask or plays out his mythology in a ritual, "the man of the archaic societies becomes conscious of himself in an 'open world' that is rich in meaning,"[37] detaching him from his narrow environment.[38] For if the visual and verbal arts are not "the vessels of spiritual revelation," they fail as art and become mere "things."[39] But it is the very nature and power of the metaphor that keep art and mythology from becoming "things." By creating and maintaining the tension between the known and the unknown, the conscious and the unconscious, the outer and inner, the past and the present,[40] "the metaphor has the task of destroying the

4

rigid reduction and limitations of the word"[41] and of
bringing two images together in a process[42] that remains
"eternally alive and universally accessible;"[43] yet it
must, as David Attenborough says of a Dogon sculpture, "be
understood in its own terms."[44]

   Clearly then, "images, symbols and myths are not
irresponsible creations of the psyche; they respond to a
need and fulfill a function, that of bringing to light the
most hidden modalities of being."[45] "Reaching into depths
into which our daily life with its various rituals can
scarcely follow,"[46] they capture the essence of the human
condition and force us to realize that the human race cannot
be divided into "primitives" and moderns; there is a unity
in the structure of humanity and no one group can be
considered inferior to another.[47] "The needs, aspirations,
and longings of mankind are similar,"[48] and as we
investigate the various manifestations of the human attempt
to understand the basic phenomena of life through the
metaphorical expression of insights, both visually in art
and verbally in mythology, we will find that they speak to
all people in "a language of vision which may tell us things
about ourselves . . . that words alone cannot touch."[49]

FOOTNOTES

1. See Genesis 1:26 and 2:19, The Bible, Revised
Standard Version. The former makes clear that this is God's
intention in setting this task, as in 2:19.

2. Bernard J. F. Lonergan, S. J., "Reality, Myth,
Symbol," Myth, Symbol, and Reality, ed. Alan M. Olson, vol.
I of the Boston University Studies in Philosophy and
Religion, ed. Leroy S. Rouner (Notre Dame, Indiana:
University of Notre Dame Press, 1980), p. 33.
　　See Barbara C. Sproul, Primal Myths, Creating the World
(San Francisco: Harper & Row, 1979), p. 19, who points out
that even the gods create by "naming."

3. Bob Samples, The Metaphoric Mind: A Celebration of
Creative Consciousness (Reading, Massachusetts:
Addison-Wesley Publishing Company, Inc., 1976), p, 157.

4. Paul S. Wingert, Primitive Art: Its Traditions and
Styles (New York: New American Library, 1962), p. 30.

5. Joshua C. Taylor, "Two Visual Excursions," The
Language of Images, ed. W. J. T. Mitchell (Chicago: The
University of Chicago Press, 1980), p. 31.

6. Mircea Eliade, Images and Symbols, trans. Philip
Mairet (Kansas City, Missouri: Sheed Andrews and McMeel,
1961), pp. 55-56.

7. Marie-Louise von Franz, Patterns of Creativity
Mirrored in Creation Myths (Zürich: Spring Publications,
1978), p. 5.

8. Harold H. Oliver, "Relational Ontology and
Hermeneutics," Myth, Symbol, and Reality, ed. Alan M.
Olson, vol. I of the Boston University Studies in Philosophy
and Religion, ed. Leroy S. Rouner (Notre Dame, Indiana:
University of Notre Dame Press, 1980), p. 78.

9. Sproul, p. 11.
　　See also Ladislas Segy, Masks of Black Africa (New York:
Dover Publications, 1976), p. 15. Segy discusses the stages
by which inner images emerge from rituals, change to
concepts, and become "externalized and concretized in
cultural objects" which we consider art today.

    10. Jacques Waardenburg, "Symbolic Aspects of Myth,"
Myth, Symbol, and Reality, ed. Alan M. Olson, vol. I of the
Boston University Studies in Philosophy and Religion, ed.
Leroy S. Rouner (Notre Dame, Indiana: University of Notre
Dame Press, 1980), p. 64.
    See also Alan W. Watts, "Foreword" to Charles H. Long,
Alpha: The Myths of Creation (Toronto, Canada: Collier
Books, 1969), p. xi, where Watts shows that by answering
questions, myths become the phenomena of cultures.

    11. David Attenborough, The Tribal Eye (London: British
Broadcasting Corporation, 1976), p. 140.

    12. Segy, p. 8.

    13. J. C. H. King, Portrait Masks from the Northwest
Coast of America (London: Thames and Hudson, 1979), p. 6.

    14. John Pemberton, "Eshu-Elegba: The Yoruba Trickster
God," African Arts, October, 1975, p. 66.

    15. Philip Freund, Myths of Creation (Levittown, New
Jersey: Transatlantic Arts, 1975), p. 233.

    16. Gregory Bateson, Steps to an Ecology of Mind; quoted
in Samples, p. ix.

    17. Segy, p. 8.

    18. Sproul, p. 16.

    19. Kees W. Bolle, The Freedom of Man in Myth
(Nashville, Tennessee: Vanderbilt University Press, 1968),
p. 5.

    20. Waardenburg, p. 53.

    21. Dorothy Jean Ray, Eskimo Masks: Art and Ceremony
(Seattle University of Washington Press, 1975), p. 10.

    22. Bolle, p. 89.

    23. Eliade, p. 13.

    24. W. J. T. Mitchell, "Spatial Form in Literature:
Toward a General Theory," The Language of Images, ed. W. J. T.
Mitchell (Chicago: The University of Chicago Press, 1980),
p. 296.

25. von Franz, p. 11.

26. Waardenburg, p. 54.

27. Ernst Cassirer, Language and Myth, trans. Susanne K. Langer (New York: Dover Publications, 1946), p. 98.

28. Elizabeth Abel, "Redefining the Sister Arts: Baudelaire's Response to the Art of Delacroix," The Language of Images, ed. W. J. T. Mitchell (Chicago: The University of Chicago Press, 1980), p. 41.
    Robert A. Lowie, Primitive Religion (New York: Liveright Publishing, 1948), pp. 267–268, suggests that the visual or artistic version tends to influence the mythology while Giulio Carlo Argan states that "myth is tied to form, and art is the expression of a mythic conception of the world." "Ideology and Iconology," The Language of Images, ed. W. J. T. Mitchell (Chicago: The University of Chicago Press, 1980), p. 16.

29. metonymic: using the name of one thing for that of another of which it is an attribute or with which it is associated.

30. Ernest B. Gilman, "Word and Image in Quarles' Emblemes," The Language of Images, ed. W. J. T. Mitchell (Chicago: The University of Chicago Press, 1980), p. 63.

31. Joseph Campbell, Myths to Live By (New York: The Viking Press, 1972), p. 31.
    Specific illustrations of various metaphoric images and an explicit discussion of the ability of metaphor to transcend the mundane and profane by creatively expressing insight into the basic phenomena of life will be developed in the body of this paper; see outline on pages 87–88.

32. Ian G. Barbour, Myths, Models and Paradigms: A Comparative Study in Science and Religion (New York: Harper & Row 1976), p. 13.

33. Segy, p. 10.

34. See pp. 1–2 above.

35. Waardenburg, p. 44.

36. Waardenburg, p. 43.

37. Eliade, p. 178.

38. Martin Foss, Symbol and Metaphor in Human Experience (Lincoln, Nebraska: University of Nebraska Press, 1949), p. 146.

39. Foss, p. 111.
See also Máscaras Mexicanas: de la Colección del Ing. Victor José Moya (Mexico City: Dirección de Museos del Instituto Nacional de Antropología e Historia, 1974), p. 15: "en muchas ocasiones la elaboración de la máscara es parte del ritual y requiere que el individual esté en un estado de pureza física y espiritual."

40. Bart McDowell, for example, discusses the artifacts that are used in Mexico today, such as those used in celebrating the Day of the Dead in terms of their ability to "retain a strong Aztec atmosphere," combining past and present in a single image by which the society can come to terms with death. "The Aztecs," National Geographic, December, 1980, p. 751.

41. Foss, p. 120.

42. See Foss, p. 171.

43. Eliade, p. 173.

44. Attenborough, p. 140.
Charles H. Long, Alpha: The Myths of Creation (Toronto, Canada: Collier Books, 1969), p. 222, also makes the point that it is important to know "the mythological symbols within a particular civilization," but Jung would argue that symbols should be regarded as universal and archetypal; see Carl Gustav Jung, Four Archetypes, trans. R. F. C. Hull, in the Bollingen Series (Princeton, New Jersey: Princeton University Press, 1973), pp. 3–5.

45. Eliade, p. 12.

46. Foss, p. 110.

47. Bolle, p. xiii.

48. Wingert, p. 72.

49. Mitchell, pp. 298–299; a reference to Bachelard's work.

BIBLIOGRAPHY

Abel, Elizabeth. "Redefining the Sister Arts: Baudelaire's Response to the Art of Delacroix." The Language of Images. Ed. W. J. T. Mitchell. Chicago: The University of Chicago Press, 1980. Pp. 37–58.

Argan, Giulio Carlo. "Ideology and Iconology." The Language of Images. Ed. W. J. T. Mitchell. Chicago: The University of Chicago Press, 1980. Pp. 15–23.

Attenborough, David. The Tribal Eye. London: British Broadcasting Corporation, 1976.

Barbour, Ian G. Myths, Models and Paradigms: A Comparative Study in Science and Religion. New York: Harper and Row, 1976.

Bolle, Kees W. The Freedom of Man in Myth. Nashville, Tennessee: Vanderbilt University Press, 1968.

Campbell, Joseph. Myths to Live By. New York: The Viking Press, 1972.

Cassirer, Ernst. Language and Myth. Trans. Susanne K. Langer. New York: Dover Publications, 1946.

Eliade, Mircea. Images and Symbols. Trans. Philip Mairet. Kansas City, Missouri: Sheed Andrews and McMeel, 1961.

Foss, Martin. Symbol and Metaphor in Human Experience. Lincoln, Nebraska: University of Nebraska Press, 1949.

Freund, Philip. Myths of Creation. Levittown, New Jersey: Transatlantic Arts, 1975.

Genesis. The Bible. Revised Standard Version.

Gilman, Ernest B. "Word and Image in Quarles' Emblemes." The Language of Images. Ed. W. J. T. Mitchell. Chicago: The University of Chicago Press, 1980. Pp. 59–84.

Jung, Carl Gustav. Four Archetypes. Trans. R. F. C. Hull. In the Bollingen Series. Princeton, New Jersey: Princeton University Press, 1973.

King, J. C. H. Portrait Masks from the Northwest Coast of America. London: Thames and Hudson, 1979.

9

10

Lonergan, Bernard J. F., S.J. "Reality, Myth, Symbol."
     Myth, Symbol, and Reality. Ed. Alan M. Olson. Vol. I of
     The Boston University Studies in Philosophy and
     Religion. Ed. Leroy S. Rouner. Notre Dame, Indiana:
     University of Notre Dame Press, 1980. Pp. 31–37.

Long, Charles H. Alpha: The Myths of Creation. Toronto,
     Canada: Collier Books, 1969.

Lowie, Robert A. Primitive Religion. New York: Liveright
     Publishing, 1948.

Máscaras Mexicanas: de la Colección del Ing. Victor José
     Moya. Mexico City: Dirección de Museos del Instituto
     Nacional de Antropología e Historia, 1974.

McDowell, Bart. "The Aztecs." National Geographic,
     December, 1980, pp. 704–752.

Mitchell, W. J. T. "Spatial Form in Literature: Toward a
     General Theory." The Language of Images. Ed. W. J. T.
     Mitchell. Chicago: The University of Chicago Press,
     1980. Pp. 271–299.

Oliver, Harold H. "Relational Ontology and Hermeneutics."
     Myth, Symbol, and Reality. Ed. Alan M. Olson. Vol. I of
     The Boston University Studies in Philosophy and
     Religion. Ed. Leroy S. Rouner. Notre Dame, Indiana:
     University of Notre Dame Press, 1980. pp. 69–85.

Pemberton, John. "Eshu–Elegba: The Yoruba Trickster God."
     African Arts, October, 1975, Pp. 20–27, 66–70, 90–92.

Ray, Dorothy Jean. Eskimo Masks: Art and Ceremony. Seattle,
     Washington: University of Washington Press, 1975.

Samples, Bob. The Metaphoric Mind: A Celebration of
     Creative Consciousness. Reading, Massachusetts:
     Addison–Wesley Publishing Company, Inc., 1976.

Segy, Ladislas. Masks of Black Africa. New York: Dover
     Publications, 1976.

Sproul, Barbara C. Primal Myths: Creating the World. San
     Francisco: Harper & Row, 1979.

11

Taylor, Joshua C. "Two Visual Excursions." The Language of Images. Ed. W. J. T. Mitchell. Chicago: The University of Chicago Press, 1980. Pp. 25-36.

von Franz, Marie-Louise. Patterns of Creativity Mirrored in Creation Myths. Zürich: Spring Publications, 1978.

Waardenburg, Jacques. "Symbolic Aspects of Myth." Myth, Symbol, and Reality. Ed. Alan M. Olson. Vol. I of The Boston University Studies in Philosophy and Religion. Ed. Leroy S. Rouner. Notre Dame, Indiana: Unversity of Notre Dame Press, 1980. Pp. 41-68.

Watts, Alan. "Foreword" to Charles H. Long, Alpha: The Myths of Creation. Toronto, Canada: Collier Books, 1969. Pp. xi-xii.

Wingert, Paul S. Primitive Art: Its Traditions and Styles. New York: New American Library, 1962.

PLAGIARISM:
A STEP TO AVOID*

The only problem of composition that is unique to the research paper is this: you must use and work with the ideas and words of other scholars. Before you are ready for this privilege and its attendant responsibility, you must understand and remember that an idea, though not a tangible article, is just as much the property of another as that person's car or clothes; often it is much more valuable. You must not use it without properly acknowledging your indebtedness. This acknowledgement, far from weakening your paper, will in fact add value and authority to your writing.

If every student understood clearly what plagiarism is, the following illustrations would not be necessary. However, the question of what is honest and what is dishonest use of source material is one that plagues many students; many of the unwary and uninformed have suffered serious consequences academically. As with the entire philosophical question of honesty, there are various degrees of plagiarism. If these examples and your own conscience are inadequate guides, consult the person who is guiding your work on your research paper.

---

*The illustrations for this section are based on the preface reproduced on pages 45-46. It is also reproduced as part of the explanation for the paraphrase (pages 104-107) at the end of this section on plagiarism.

WORD-FOR-WORD PLAGIARISM

I was attracted to mythology because of my fascination with the dramatic action of the stories and the feeling of magic that enters the world in which that action happens. But gradually I realized that on another level those marvelous tales were metaphorical expressions of essential aspects of the human condition. Each social group had obviously developed a body of myths by which it could understand the basic experiences of its existence, such as creation, death, and nature. Although these mythological stories might not be literally true, they do by analogy capture the essential truth both of the basic nature of being and of the society's world view. Von Franz says that when people attempt to explain the unknown, they are likely to depend on imagery from what they do know or on ar·hetypal images which come out of their own inner experiences. Later I realized that these images are also found in primitive art. Mitchell explains that visual representation is not radically distinct from language, and Elizabeth Abel claims that the underlying concepts of myth and art are similar in that both express a common inner source in which the subject matter changes but the nature is the same. I was challenged to investigate the common denominators of the verbal and visual expressions of these insights and to do a comparative study of their metaphoric forms.

COMMENT: Transposing or substituting a few words will not create a paraphrase. In this example, after saying "I was attracted to" instead of "My earliest attraction," the writer of this nearly verbatim piece of plagiarism simply used different words or reworded some short phrases: "was based on" was changed to "because of my"; "narratives" became "stories"; "pervades" became "enters"; "aura" became "feeling"; "takes place" became "happens"; "mythology" became "body of myths," etc. In two other instances the order of the words was reversed: "creation, nature, and death" became "creation, death, and nature" and the order of "basic nature of being" was reversed with "society's world view." Both the paraphrased passage and the directly quoted passages so carefully documented in the original were used here without any documentation. As written, this passage is almost purely a word-for-word copy of the source, retaining even the sentence structure and organization of the original. Even the use of a footnote could not save this paragraph from being condemned.

PATCHWORK PLAGIARISM

I was attracted to <u>mythology</u> because of my childhood <u>fascination with</u> <u>the</u> <u>dramatic</u> <u>action</u> <u>of the</u> magic-like stories they contain. Now, in college <u>I</u> <u>realize</u> <u>that</u> there is <u>another</u> <u>level</u> to the <u>marvelous</u> <u>tales;</u> they are <u>metaphorical</u> <u>expressions</u> <u>of</u> <u>essential</u> <u>aspects</u> of the <u>human</u> <u>condition.</u> All cultures seem to have <u>a</u> <u>mythology</u> that helps them <u>understand</u> <u>the</u> basic <u>experiences</u> <u>of</u> their <u>existence.</u> Even though many of these myths could never be scientifically proved, they do seem to parallel the meaning <u>of</u> a society's belief. **When people <u>attempt to explain the unknown, they</u> use <u>archetypal images</u> <u>which</u> <u>come out of inner experiences.</u> *I <u>realized too</u> that some of these <u>images</u> can be <u>found</u> in <u>primitive art</u> which <u>is not radically</u> <u>distinct</u> <u>from</u> <u>language</u> which shows <u>that</u> <u>the</u> <u>underlying</u> concepts <u>of</u> <u>myth</u> <u>and</u> <u>art</u> <u>are</u> <u>similar</u> because they <u>both</u> <u>express</u> the same <u>subject</u> <u>matter</u> which <u>changes</u> <u>but</u> whose <u>nature</u> <u>is</u> <u>the</u> <u>same.</u> My paper will <u>investigate</u> <u>the</u> <u>common</u> <u>denominators</u> <u>of</u> <u>the</u> <u>verbal</u> <u>and</u> <u>visual</u> <u>expressions</u> <u>of</u> these ideas <u>and</u> I will compare <u>their</u> <u>metaphoric</u> <u>forms.</u>

COMMENT: Changing a single word in a passage otherwise quoted verbatim does not produce a paraphrase. The starred passage (**) would still need to be in quotation marks and footnoted; the changes you make within a quoted passage should go in square brackets, as do all editorial changes and additions; ellipsis marks are used to indicate omissions from the source being quoted. Thus the starred (*) sentence above should be: I realized too that some of these images can be "found in primitive art . . . [which] is not radically distinct from language" according to Mitchell which shows, Elizabeth Abel says "that the underlying concepts of myth and art are similar." The footnote number would then follow the quotation marks.

When whole phrases are lifted out and are put into a framework of your own wording or into a "different" arrangement of the original, the result is also called plagiarism. In the example above, the underlined phrases are lifted verbatim from the original. Though you would never be expected to put quotation marks merely around such phrases as "I realized," "when people attempt to explain," or "inner experiences," since they are part of our common idiom, you could not write such a sentence as the one marked ** above and call it your own. This "rearrangement" is not really a paraphrasing. The sentence preceding it might be called a paraphrase but would still need a footnote; it is very awkwardly stated because the implications of the idea expressed were obviously not very clear to the writer. If all the underlined phrases were in quotation marks, the paragraph would resemble an old-fashioned patchwork quilt. It would also be quite unreadable and certainly not original. Not only is Markman not given credit for her work in the plagiarized version but the sources *she* carefully documented have also been plagiarized.

"LIFTING OUT THE PERFECT PHRASES"

The aura of magic that pervades mythology and my early fascination with the dramatic action of the stories stimulated my interest in myths. That they were metaphorical expressions explaining creation, nature, and death was clear to me as I became more sophisticated. As metaphors they could by analogy capture the essential truth that was close to each social group so that it could understand the basic experiences of its existence. The imagery, when people attempt to explain the unknown comes from their own worldly experiences or from archetypal images that are part of their inner psyches as we find from illustrations found on maps of antiquity. Since art is not radically distinct from language,[1] I would like to investigate the common denominators of the insights of primitive people as they expressed them verbally in their myths and visually in their art to see if the nature is the same and to study the metaphoric forms of each of them.

---

[1] W. J. T. Mitchell, "Spatial Form in Literature: Toward a General Theory," *The Language of Images*, ed. W. J. T. Mitchell (Chicago: The University of Chicago Press, 1980), p. 296.

COMMENT: Though more subtle and clever, this kind of plagiarism is similar to the patchwork illustration above. The "perfect phrases" irresistible to the writer here are underlined so you may spot them easily. However, the order in which they appear is often altered.

The words that are underlined with wavy lines might be called paraphrases but could not be used without footnotes. The phrasing "the insights of primitive people as they expressed them verbally in their myths and visually in their art" certainly reflect Markman's ideal and, though paraphrased, must be documented as having been quoted from Markman.

Two other serious errors were made in this paragraph:

1. Mitchell was cited in a footnote as if his article were a source used by the writer. (If you did not read the article, you may not cite it.)

2. Not content with "lifting" material from the Preface, the writer has copied the words "found on maps of antiquity" from Marie-Louise von Franz so carefully quoted in Markman's footnotes.

PARAPHRASE

PREFACE

My earliest attraction to mythology was based on a fascination with the

Myths fascinate on several levels. They are

dramatic action of the narratives and the aura of magic that pervades the

imaginative stories that have magic appeal.

world in which that action takes place. But gradually I realized that on

Moreover, the sophisticated scholar can see that

another level those marvelous tales were metaphorical expressions of

by their imagery they are able to capture the essence

essential aspects of the human condition. Each social group had obviously

of some of humanity's most important experiences,

developed a mythology by which it could understand the basic experiences

including how people came into being, their

of its existence, such as creation, nature, and death. Although their

relationship to the world around them, and death.

mythological stories might not be literally true, they do by analogy capture

Apparently every society develops a body of myths in order

the essential truth both of the society's world view and of the basic nature of

to understand these basic mysteries of life. Even though

being. Von Franz says that when people attempt to explain the unknown,

there is no way to prove anything scientifically. the central

they are likely to depend on imagery from what they do know or on

metaphors of the stories do express the essence of

archetypal images which come out of their own inner experiences.[1]

truth about the human condition. In her book about

Later I realized that these images are also found in primitive art. Mitchell

creation myths, for example, Marie Louise von Franz

explains that visual representation is "not radically distinct from language,"[2]

says that the metaphors are based on imagery either

and Elizabeth Abel contends that the underlying concepts of myth and art

from people's own experiences or from the primordial images of their psyches, and both W.J.T. Mitchell and Elizabeth Abel suggest that the same imagery

are similar in that both express a "common inner source whose subject

is often found in art forms even though the actual

matter changes but whose nature is the same."[3] I was challenged to

subject may not be the same. ② A comparison of the

investigate the common denominators of the verbal and visual expressions

two forms of expression would result in a very

of these insights and to do a comparative study of their metaphoric forms.

valuable study to discover the "truths" expressed in the metaphoric imagery that primitive societies have left us in their art and in their mythology.

[1] Marie-Louise von Franz, *Patterns of Creativity Mirrored in Creation Myths* (Zürich: Spring Publications, 1978), p. 5. Von Franz bases her conclusions on the images she has found on maps of antiquity.

[2] W. J. T. Mitchell, "Spatial Form in Literature: Toward a General Theory," *The Language of Images,* ed. W. J. T. Mitchell (Chicago: The University of Chicago Press, 1980), p. 296. Mitchell reinforces his point with a quote from Ludwig Wittgenstein's *Philosophical Investigations:* "A picture held us captive. And we could not get outside it, for it lay in our language and language seemed to repeat it to us inexorably" (Mitchell, p. 271).

[3] Elizabeth Abel, "Redefining the Sister Arts: Baudelaire's Response to the Art of Delacroix," *The Language of Images,* ed. W. J. T. Mitchell (Chicago: The University of Chicago Press, 1980), p. 41.

[1] *Marie-Louise von Franz, Patterns of Creativity Mirrored in Creation Myths (Zürich: Spring Publications, 1978), p.5; quoted in Roberta H. Markman, "The Metaphoric Vision in Mythology and Art," unpublished master's thesis, Department of Comparative Literature, California State University, Long Beach, 1982, p. iv.*

> [2] W.J.T. Mitchell, "Spatial Form in Literature: Toward a General Theory" and Elizabeth Abel, "Redefining the Sister Arts: Baudelaire's Response to the Art of Delacroix," both in *The Language of Images*, ed. W.J.T. Mitchell (Chicago: The University of Chicago Press, 1980), pp. 41, 271; quoted in Roberta H. Markman, "The Metaphoric Vision in Mythology and Art," unpublished master's thesis, Department of Comparative Literature, California State University, Long Beach, 1982, p. iv.

COMMENT: This is a paraphrase, for the writer here has followed the source, sentence by sentence and idea by idea but has used his own words. There is value in doing this (see the reasons listed above card F on page 52), but remember that you must not alter the sense of the original.

Also remember: although the words in a paraphrase (or a précis, q.v.) may truly be your own, the thoughts and opinions are not; therefore you must acknowledge your indebtedness to the thinking of the original writer by one of three methods:

1. Put a footnote number after the passage and in a footnote give the source. See STEP 9.

2. Use an informal in-text documentation. See pages 71, 81.

3. Assuming that you have already given a footnote for this paraphrased preface, give the author credit in a phrase such as "to paraphrase Markman's thesis . . ." or "As Markman says in her Preface . . ." and in a footnote give simply the page number. (See 7 on page 81.)

REMEMBER: Of the four examples above, only the paraphrase could be used without quotation marks, and even it would require documentation in a footnote. THE OTHER EXAMPLES WOULD BE CALLED PLAGIARISM *EVEN WITH* DOCUMENTATION.

THE LIBRARY: A STEP TO MASTER

USING THE LIBRARY FOR BOOKS AND OTHER COMMUNICATIONS MEDIA

The library is the most valuable storehouse of information on almost every subject for anyone doing research. It is essential, therefore, to become familiar with the tools in your library and to make use of as many of them as your time affords.

1. **The Card Catalog**

   All students should consider the card catalog as their most valuable index. When you locate a card for a book you want, it is essential to copy the entire call number accurately, since it is the most important mark of identification for locating any book.

2. **The Reference Rooms**

   Become familiar with the basic reference texts in your particular subject. The periodical indexes, special indexes, bibliographies, and special encyclopedias (see pages 117-122) are in the reference room of the library. Ask at the information desk to find out whether or not the library has reference rooms for different subjects or whether all references may be found in one place.

3. Special Sections

In larger libraries there are often special rooms for collections of bibliographies, circulating art prints and slides, periodicals, audiovisual aids, phonograph records, tapes, pamphlets, rare books and folios, newspapers, reserve books, dissertations and other unpublished manuscripts, maps, and other special materials, each of which may have its own separate catalog or listing; hence it is important for you to check these various sections in your particular library as you search for relevant materials.

4. Films and Filmstrips

Many libraries afford students the opportunity to view films and filmstrips; often, arrangements must be made in advance for this privilege.

5. Pamphlets

Pamphlets are a valuable source of additional current information on any subject. Often they are circulated, although they will not be found listed in the card catalog. Even a little pamphlet can contain great ideas.

6. Microfilms and Microfiche

Microfilms and microfiche have enabled libraries to store and mail copies of books that would not otherwise be available. Microfilm reading machines are easy to use and very interesting; you may even find that the machine helps you to keep awake between pages. Microfiche require the use of a microprint reading machine which is also simple to handle; it enables a library to have an entire work on a single card. In a busy library, be sure to make arrangements in advance for the use of these miraculous machines.

7. Records and Tapes

Although many students may not be aware of it, music is not the only material that is available on phonograph records and tapes. You should check these for recordings of lectures and readings on every subject, since some of these may not be available in other media.

8. Newspapers

All issues of the most important newspapers are available on microfilm; they are often listed in the holding file of a periodical room.

9. Periodicals

Many periodical indexes are available in the reference room of the library. (See pages 16-17.) After you have found the source of an article that interests you, check the holding file of periodicals to find out if the periodical you need is available in your library. Issues of periodicals published in the same year have the same volume number and are eventually bound together in the same volume; so if you need several issues with the same volume number (of a bound periodical), you need to ask or look for only one bound volume. Often you can arrange to borrow those that are not available in your library, but this entails using the interlibrary loan service discussed under 12d below.

10. Picture File

Mounted magazine pictures, commercially prepared study prints, and pictorial maps are often available through the library. These can be valuable aids in many areas of research. Art prints are often available on loan for you to enjoy at home or in your own room for a considerable length of time.

11. Stack Privileges

Depending on the regulations of each individual library, some students have the privilege of going directly to the library stacks, a privilege which will enable them to look at all the works in sections (or call numbers) related to their research subjects. If you have this privilege, this chance to browse will reveal material that you might not have found in the card catalog. It is important to use the indexes of the various books that seem relevant in order to ascertain their value to your project.

12. Special Services

Your library is often equipped to offer you many special services:

a. Renewal of books you have not finished using,
b. "Holding" a book that someone else has taken out of the library. If you request a "hold" on a book, your library will notify you when it is returned to the library and before it is returned to the library. It is important to respond quickly to a notice that a "hold" book is waiting for you because your library may have a time limit on this service.
c. Xerox or copying machines are usually available for you to use in copying or duplicating material from a book in the library. Be aware

of the copyright laws, however, as only a limited amount of material is legally available for copying.

d. Most libraries subscribe to an interlibrary loan service which makes available most of the world's materials, even those not in your library. Materials obtained through this service are usually borrowed for a very limited time, so it is wise to find out how long it will take for the material to reach you and how long you may keep it.

There are, of course, many ways in which you will encounter the names of books that you think will be valuable for your research. Usually you will find them in bibliographies by other researchers or referred to in footnotes or appendixes in your sources. Then you should check the *National Union Catalog,* which your librarian will have and with which you can locate books in hundreds of American libraries. Through the interlibrary loan service you can usually obtain the books you need. Winifred Gregory's *Union List of Serials,* though not quite as complete or up to date, also serves the same purpose: it helps you locate periodicals in other libraries. You can find films listed in the *Union List of Microfilms* and *Newspapers on Microfilms.*

e. Typewriters are available for student use in most libraries and are usually coin-operated.

13. The Reference Librarian

The reference librarian is always a busy person, but when all else fails he or she is the one who is professionally trained to help you locate materials and use the library to its greatest potential. Solicit the help of the reference librarian only after you have tried to help yourself, but do not hesitate to ask for help when you honestly need it.

APPENDICES

RESEARCH TERMS DEFINED

Research writing, like any other specialized activity, has its own jargon. The following are terms frequently used by people in discussing research:

abridgment: a condensation of the author's original work (expurgated text).
acknowledgment: recognition made of indebtedness to another.
annotated bibliography: a bibliography with comments about each source, telling how inclusive it is, how valuable it is, what the author does and what his or her purpose is, and so on.
authority: a writer whose work and opinions are generally accepted as final and reliable.
autobiography: the writer's own account of his or her life.
bibliography: a list of books, articles, and other material about a single subject, idea, person, and so forth.
biography: a writer's account of the life story of another. There are three types: straight, fictional, and critical.
brackets: the punctuation marks [ ] used only within a quoted passage to enclose additions in your own words (called editorial comment, insertion, or interpolation) explaining a word or giving information needed by the reader.
Brackets may be drawn in black ink if the typewriter has no brackets.

NEVER use unnecessary brackets: "He [Aristotle] wrote an early definition of tragedy"; simply write this: Aristotle "wrote an early definition of tragedy." Parentheses are different and have a different function.

card catalog: a card file listing alphabetically all books in a library.
Usually each book is listed under author, book title, and subject.

cross reference: words or symbols which refer the reader to other places where information about an idea may be found.
Cross references are used in card catalogs, footnotes, indexes, and bibliographies.

compile (compilation, compiler): to combine related material. The one who does the combining is a compiler; the result is a compilation.

dedication: a page of tribute by the writer to one he or she admires or feels indebted to or wants to honor.

dissertation: a long, involved, and formal exposition on some serious or scholarly subject.
In academic circles, the word is usually reserved for those papers written by a candidate for a doctorate; the word *thesis* indicates the paper written by a candidate for the master's degree.

document: to acknowledge indebtedness for an idea or fact. It is necessary to document the source of any critical opinion (and some facts); see the section on footnotes, STEP 9.

ellipsis: an omission within quoted material indicated by three periods with a space before, after, and between periods (. . .).
The ellipsis marks may indicate the omission of a single word or of whole sentences, but you must never omit words which would change the essential, intended meaning of the quoted material. It is illogical to use an ellipsis to open or to close a quoted passage; hence it would never come immediately after an opening quotation mark nor immediately before the closing quotation mark unless you wish to emphasize the omission of material before or after the passage quoted; it should be used only to show an omission within a quoted passage. Use a fourth period only before a new sentence which begins after an ellipsis within the quoted passage.

file: frequently misused as a substitute for the proper term *card catalog*. The word *file* is properly used to refer to some special library file such as the vertical file, which contains temporarily interesting leaflets, pamphlets, newspaper and magazine clippings, illustrations, and so on that are not permanently classified and filed but are put in standing (vertical) files and removed when the interest fades: as one librarian put it, "temporary stuff and current junk."

foreword: a note from the author at the front of a book.

Current practice reveals that there is some confusion about the exact distinctions between the sections called *foreword, preface,* and *introduction;* however, by whatever name it may be called, this section sets forth an explanation by the author of his or her intended purpose and reason for writing as well as any information or background that might be needed by the reader.

interpolate: to insert an idea or material or information where it should logically go in the organization of the writing.

introduction: a section that follows the table of contents and introduces the work that follows. See *foreword* above.

pagination: the system for numbering pages of a manuscript or book.

parentheses: the punctuation marks ( ) used to enclose your own explanatory material or words interpolated into a sentence or phrase of your own.

Brackets (q.v.) enclose material more foreign to the context than that put in parentheses; avoid the overuse of either.

plagiarism: a literary word for the thievery of style, ideas, or phrasing. Plagiarism ranges from the theft of a single word to the deliberate copying (without quotation marks) of a whole passage; it can be avoided by careful note taking and footnoting (q.v.); everything not documented must be your own original idea and phrasing. You are not writing original sentences of your own if you merely arrange into a new order or sentence pattern some select phrases and sentences taken without quotation marks from your sources. See section entitled "Plagiarism: A Step to Avoid," pages 100-107.

primary source: the literature, the work, manuscript, journal, letters, and so on as originally written.

A secondary source is a work written about an original source; a primary source in connection with one subject might be a secondary source in connection with another subject.

For example, a novel by Faulkner would be a primary source for a paper about Faulkner or the novel in America and so on; a Master's thesis on Faulkner would be a primary source for a paper on the writing of theses in American colleges and universities, but it would be a secondary source for a paper on Faulkner.

preface: a note from the author which comes before (some put it after) the table of contents or outline.

The preface is frequently followed by a page of acknowledgments; see *foreword* above.

rough draft: the first and any subsequent writing before the paper is put in final form.

Rough drafts are subject to drastic and sometimes numerous revisions.

reference or reference book: any source being read for information.
The number and quality of your references will in large measure determine the quality of your finished paper.

scan: to make a cursory reading of material in order to evaluate it and decide how to read it.

secondary source: a criticism or evaluation of an original piece of writing. See *primary source* above.

slug (label, tag): the label on a notecard written above the top line and immediately after the identifying symbol.
It may be taken from or may suggest ideas for the outline units.

thesis: the simple statement of opinion which the entire work is designed to support.
See complete explanation and examples in STEP 3.

LIBRARY CLASSIFICATION SYSTEMS

The "call numbers" on the card in the card catalog and on the backs of books usually follow the Library of Congress system or the Dewey decimal system. The former is more often used by college libraries and large collections.

THE LIBRARY OF CONGRESS CLASSIFICATION SYSTEM

The Library of Congress system divides all branches of knowledge into twenty-one main groups which are designated by letters of the alphabet. Then each branch is further divided by the addition of letters and Arabic numerals, permitting endless combinations. The twenty-one groups are:

A   General Works-Polygraphy
B   Philosophy-Religion
C   History-Auxiliary Sciences
D   History-Topography (except America)
E-F   American History and Topography
G   Geography-Anthropology
H   Social Sciences
J   Political Science
K   Law
L   Education
M   Music

N   Fine Arts
P   Language and Literature
Q   Science
R   Medicine
S   Agriculture-Plant and Animal Husbandry
T   Technology
U   Military Science
V   Naval Science
Z   Bibliography and Library Science

To illustrate the subdivision of an area of knowledge, "P" designates the Language and Literature category which subdivides:

P   Philology and Linguistics: General
PA   Greek and Latin Philology and Literature
PB   Celtic Language and Literature
PC   Romance Languages (French, Spanish, Italian)
PD   Germanic Languages

THE DEWEY DECIMAL SYSTEM

All branches of knowledge are divided into ten numbered parts according to hundreds, which are then further divided into specific areas of knowledge. The number on the first line is the call number; below it are other lines indicating the code used for author, a particular work, the edition, the number of copies on hand, and so on. The numbers below indicate ways the number on the first line may appear.

000 General Works
100 Philosophy
200 Religion
300 Social Sciences
400 Language (Philology)
500 Pure Science
600 Useful Arts
700 Fine Arts
800 Literature
900 History

These parts are further divided; the second number in the 800's indicates the country or language of the literature.

810   American Literature in English
820   English and Old English
830   Germanic Literature
840   French, Provençal, Catalan
850   Italian, Rumanian
860   Spanish, Portuguese

REFERENCE MATERIALS AND GUIDES

Most research will start in the reference room of your library; there you will find many volumes written not to be read but to be used as guides to general and to specialized articles and books about all fields of knowledge. These indexes and general reference books are guides only; they do not contain material you will read; they will not be a part of your bibliography. Quite literally, they are tools which you must learn to use, and no amount of explanation will replace experience and an active imagination. Hence the list below contains only the names of a few reference guides and is not annotated.

GENERAL WORKS

There are numerous atlases, dictionaries, and encyclopedias which are too familiar to the average student to need listing here.

GUIDES TO REFERENCE SOURCES

Barton, Mary N., comp. *Reference Books, a Brief Guide for Students and Other Users of the Library,* 7th ed. Baltimore: Enoch Pratt Free Library, 1970.

Hillard, James M. *Where to Find What: A Handbook to Reference Service.* Metuchen, New Jersey: Scarecrow Press, 1975.

Mark, Linda, ed. *Reference Sources.* 3 vols. Ann Arbor, Michigan: The Pierian Press, 1979.

Murphey, Robert W. *How and Where to Look It Up: A Guide to Standard Sources of Information.* New York: McGraw-Hill, 1958.

Sheehy, Eugene Paul, comp. *Guide to Reference Books,* 9th ed. Chicago: American Library Association, 1976. Supplement, 1980.

Vitale, Philip H. *Basic Tools of Research,* 3rd ed. Woodbury, New York: Barron's, 1975.

NOTE: The above guides give more detailed information about possible sources than you will find in some indexes (such as those that follow)

BIBLIOGRAPHIES AND SUPPLEMENTS TO THE CARD CATALOG

Bibliographic Index: A Cumulative Bibliography of Bibliographies. New York: H. W. Wilson, 1934 to date.

The Cumulative Book Index. New York: H. W. Wilson, 1928 to date. (For books in print in English prior to 1928, see *The United States Catalog,* 4th ed. New York: H. W. Wilson, 1928.)

Essay and General Literature Index. New York: H. W. Wilson, 1934 to date.

A Guide to the Study of the United States of America. Washington, D.C.: Library of Congress, 1960. Supplement, 1956-1965.

Monthly Catalog of United States Government Publications. Washington, D.C.: Government Printing Office, 1895 to date.

Toomey, Alice F., comp. *A World Bibliography of Bibliographies, 1964-1974.* 2 vols. Totowa, New Jersey: Rowman and Littlefield, 1977.

BIOGRAPHICAL REFERENCE BOOKS AND DICTIONARIES

Biography Index. New York: H. W. Wilson, 1946 to date.

Current Biography. New York: H. W. Wilson, 1940 to date.

Dictionary of American Biography. 22 vols., index, and supplements. New York: Scribner, 1928-1960.

Ethredge, James M., and Barbara Kopala, eds. *Contemporary Authors.* 84 vols. Detroit: Gale Research Corp., 1962 to date.

Thorne, J. O., ed. *Chamber's Biographical Dictionary,* rev. ed. New York: St. Martin's Press, 1969.

Webster's Biographical Dictionary. Springfield, Massachusetts: G. & C. Merriam, 1970.

Who's Who. New York: Macmillan, 1849 to date.

REFERENCE BOOKS AND INDEXES ON VARIOUS SUBJECTS

It is almost impossible to draw absolute lines dividing ideas and subjects, to say that one idea concerns just one and no other area of thinking; it is also impossible to define exactly the line distinguishing the subject matter in all the books in a library. The list below therefore makes arbitrary divisions for the sake of convenience.

THE FINE ARTS AND THE HUMANITIES

GENERAL WORKS

Bartlett, John. *Familiar Quotations,* 14th ed. Boston: Little, Brown, 1968.

Humanities Index. New York: H. W. Wilson, 1907 to date. (Formerly *The International Index to Periodical Literature,* 1907-1966, and *Social Sciences and Humanities Index,* 1966-1974.)

Union List of Microfilms. Cumulation 1949-1959. 2 vols. Ann Arbor, Michigan: Edwards Brothers, 1961.

ART

Art Index. New York: H. W. Wilson, 1929 to date.

Gardner, Helen. *Art Through the Ages,* 6th ed. New York: Harcourt, Brace, Jovanovich, 1975.

Index to Art Periodicals, compiled in Ryerson Library, The Art Institute of Chicago. 11 vols. Boston: G. K. Hall, 1962. Supplement, 1975.

LITERATURE, THEATER, AND FILM

Blanck, Jacob, comp. *Bibliography of American Literature.* 6 vols. New Haven: Yale University Press, 1955-1973.

Burke, W. J., and Will D. Howe. *American Authors and Books,* augmented and revised by Irving R. Weiss. New York: Crown, 1962.

Hopper, Vincent F., and Bernard D. N. Grebanier. *Bibliography of European Literature.* Woodbury, New York: Barron's, 1954.

M.L.A. Bibliography. New York: Modern Language Association of America, 1929 to date.

The National Union Catalog (motion pictures and filmstrips). Library of Congress Catalogs 1963-1967. 5 vols. Ann Arbor, Michigan: Edwards Brothers, 1967.

Ottemiller, John H. *Index to Plays in Collections,* 5th ed. Metuchen, New Jersey: Scarecrow Press, 1971.

Play Index. New York: H. W. Wilson, 1977. (Formerly *Index to Plays, 1800-1926,* comp. Ina Firkins.)

Smith, William James, ed. *Granger's Index to Poetry,* 6th ed. New York: Columbia University Press, 1973. Supplement, 1970-1977.

Watson, George, ed. *Cambridge Bibliography of English Literature,* rev. ed. 5 vols. Cambridge: Cambridge University Press, 1974-1977.

MUSIC

Duckles, Vincent. *Music Reference and Research Materials,* 2nd ed. New York: The Free Press, 1967.

Grove's Dictionary of Music and Musicians, 5th ed. 9 vols. New York: St. Martin's Press, 1954. Supplement, 1961.

Schirmer's Guide to Books on Music and Musicians. New York: Schirmer, 1951.

THE SCIENCES

GENERAL WORKS

Applied Science and Technology Index. New York: H. W. Wilson, 1958 to date. (Formerly *Industrial Arts Index,* 1913-1958).

Hawkins, Reginald R. *Scientific, Medical and Technical Books Published in the United States of America.* Washington, D.C.: National Research Council, 1958.

Jenkins, Frances Briggs. *Science Reference Sources,* 5th ed. Cambridge, Massachusetts: The MIT Press, 1969.

Sarton, George. *A Guide to the History of Science.* New York: Ronald Press, 1952.

Scientific and Technical Books in Print, 1972-1974. 3 vols. New York: R. R. Bowker, 1974.

ENGINEERING

Dalton, Blanche H. *Sources of Engineering Information.* Berkeley: University of California Press, 1948.

The Engineering Index. New York: Engineering Index, Inc., 1980 (Volume 1—1884; Volume 79—1980).

MATHEMATICS, CHEMISTRY, AND PHYSICS

Gould, Robert F., ed. *Searching the Chemical Literature.* Washington, D.C.: American Chemical Society, 1961.

Marzell, Robert E. *How to Find Chemical Information.* New York: John Wiley and Sons, 1979.

Mellon, Melvin G. *Chemical Publications,* 4th ed. New York: McGraw-Hill, 1965.

Parke, Nathan G. *Guide to the Literature of Mathematics and Physics,* 2nd ed. New York: McGraw-Hill, 1958.

THE SOCIAL SCIENCES

GENERAL WORKS

Hoselitz, Berthold F. *A Reader's Guide to the Social Sciences,* rev. ed. Glencoe, Illinois: Free Press, 1970.

Social Sciences Index. New York: H. W. Wilson, 1907 to date. (Formerly *The International Index to Periodical Literature,* 1907-1966 and *Social Sciences and Humanities Index,* 1966-1974.)

White, Carl M. *Sources of Information in the Social Sciences: A Guide to the Literature,* 2nd ed. Chicago: American Library Association, 1973.

BUSINESS AND ECONOMICS

Coman, Edwin T. *Sources of Business Information,* rev. ed. Berkeley, California: University of California Press, 1964.

Horton, Byrne J., and others. *Dictionary of Modern Economics.* Washington, D.C.: Public Affairs Press, 1948.

Manley, Marian C. *Business Information: How to Find and Use It.* New York: Harper & Brothers, 1955.

Wasserman, Paul, ed. *Encyclopedia of Business Information Sources.* 2 vols. Detroit: Gale Research Corp., 1970.

EDUCATION

Alexander, Carter, and Arvid J. Burke. *Documentation in Education.* New York: Bureau of Publications, Teachers College, Columbia University, 1967.

Education Index. New York: H. W. Wilson, 1929 to date.

Encyclopaedia of Educational Research, 4th ed. New York: Macmillan, 1969.

HISTORY, POLITICAL SCIENCE, AND SOCIOLOGY

Beers, Henry P. *Bibliographies in American History,* rev. and enl. ed. New York: Cooper Square Press, 1960.

Brock, Clifton. *The Literature of Political Science.* New York: R. R. Bowker, 1969.

Clark, George K. *Guide for Research Students Working on Historical Subjects,* 2nd ed. Cambridge, England: Cambridge University Press, 1968.

Dutcher, George Matthew, and others, eds. *Guide to Historical Literature.* New York: Macmillan, 1949. (A reissue.)

Langer, William, and others, comps. and eds. *Encyclopedia of World History,* 5th ed. Boston: Houghton Mifflin, 1972.

Statesman's Year-Book. New York: Macmillan, 1864 to date.

Will, Annadel N., ed. *C.R.I.S.: The Combined Retrospective Index to Journals in History, 1838-1974.* 11 vols. Washington, D.C.: Carrollton Press, 1977-1978.

RELIGION, PHILOSOPHY, AND PSYCHOLOGY

Baldwin, James M. *Dictionary of Philosophy and Psychology.* 3 vols. in 4. New York: Smith, 1925. (A reissue in 1949.)

Encyclopedia of Philosophy. 8 vols. New York: Macmillan, 1967.

Ferm, Vergilius. *Encyclopedia of Religion.* Paterson, New Jersey: Littlefield, Adams, and Co., 1959.

List of Books in Psychology, 3rd ed. Cambridge, Massachusetts: Harvard University Press, 1964.

Meagher, Paul Kevin and others, eds. *Encyclopedic Dictionary of Religion.* 3 vols. Washington, D.C.: Corpus Publications, 1979.

Peterson, Russell A. *A Dictionary of Philosophical Concepts.* Lake Mills, Iowa: Graphic Publishing Co., 1977.

Runes, Dagobert D. *Dictionary of Philosophy.* New York: Philosophical Library, 1942.

Warren, Howard C. *Dictionary of Psychology.* New York: Houghton Mifflin, 1934.

ABBREVIATIONS

anon.	anonymous
bk., bks.	book(s)
c., ca.	*circa:* "about"; for approximate dates (c. 1884, ca. 1884)
cf.	*confer:* "compare"; not a synonym for *see*
chap., ch., chs.	chapter(s)
col., cols.	column(s)
comp.	compiler, compiled, compiled by
ed., eds.	editor(s), edition(s), or edited by
e.g.	*exempli gratia:* "for example"
et al.	*et alii:* "and others"
et seq.	*et sequens:* "and the following" (or ff., which is shorter)
ex.	example
f., ff.	and the following page(s) (pp. 79f. or pp. 79ff.)
fig., figs.	figure(s)
ibid.	*ibidem:* "in the same place as quoted above"; refers to title in footnote immediately above; author's name not given; page given if different from the one preceding
i.e.	*id est:* "that is"; preceded by a comma and followed by a comma and list or explanation
ill., illus.	illustration; illustrated by
l., ll.	line(s)
loc. cit.	*loco citato:* "in the place cited"; refers to work fully identified in any previous footnote except the one immediately preceding; preceded by author's last name;

	never followed by a page number because *loc. cit.* means "in the same location" (page) as in last footnote referring to that source
MS (MSS)	manuscript(s); always capitalized; no period
N.B.	*nota bene:* "take notice; mark well"; always capitalized
n.d.	no date given
no., nos.	number(s)
n.p.	no place of publication (and/or no publisher) given
op. cit.	*opere citato:* "in the work cited"; preceded by author's last name and followed by page number (because *op. cit.* stands for title only); refers to work cited previously but not immediately above
p., pp.	page(s)
passim	"throughout the work, here and there"; (p. 37 et passim means p. 37 and other scattered pages; or pp. 37-42 passim)
pl., pls.	plate(s)
pseud.	pseudonym, pen name (Lewis Carroll, Mark Twain)
pt.	part
q.v.	*quod vide:* "which see"
rev.	review by; revised or revised by; revision
rpt.	reprint
sc.	scene
sec., secs.	section(s)
sic	"thus"; not an abbreviation; used within brackets to indicate that an error in quote is in the original: "It was to [*sic*] bad."
st.	stanza
tr., trans.	translator, translation, translated by
v., vv.	verse(s)
viz.	*videlicet:* "namely"; use with or without a period; usage varies
vol., vols.	volume(s); capitalize only before Roman numeral: Vol. VII; 9 vols.

ROMAN NUMERALS

I	V	X	L	C	D	M
1	5	10	50	100	500	1000

To read a number with two or more Roman numerals, start with the larger numeral and subtract what is to the left; add what is to the right.

If a numeral is between two of greater value, subtract it from the second and then add that number (the remainder) to the first:

$$MCMLXXI = 1971$$

A bar over a numeral multiplies it by 1000. Roman numerals may be written in capitals or in lower case.

$$IX = 9 \quad XXXII = 32 \quad XL = 40 \quad CL = 150$$
$$CD = 400 \quad CDV = 405$$
$$DC = 600 \quad CM = 900 \quad \overline{IV} = 4000$$

Use Roman numerals in capitals (IV, XII, CDL) when you want

to indicate volumes of books in series;
to number the acts in a play;
to number the books of a long poem (or the cantos);
to identify different people with the same name (George III);
to indicate major divisions in an outline;
to number chapters in the Bible.

Use Roman numerals in lower case (ii, iv, xii) when you want

to number all prefatory pages including outline and table of contents;
to identify scenes in a drama;
to identify verses of chapters in the Bible.

BASIC PUNCTUATION

Punctuating your research paper will be easy if you learn these basic rules that apply to the structures or patterns most frequently used in writing. If you keep the following rules in mind, especially those pertaining to the use of the comma, your paper will be clear and effective.

1. The Apostrophe

a. Use an apostrophe with an *s* to show possession (belonging to): Mary's hat, the heart's desire. *Except,* if the word ends in *s,* then add the apostrophe after the *s*: the Smiths' book (belonging to the Smith family). On occasion, for the sake of pronunciation, a word ending in *s* forms the possessive by adding *es*: the Williames book (belonging to the Williams family).

b. Use an apostrophe to show that a letter has been omitted: it's/it is; who's/who is; there's/there is.

> NOTE: Possessive pronouns have their own forms and do not require an apostrophe: mine, yours, his, their(s), its.

2. The comma

Do not use a comma unless one of the following rules apply:

a. Use a comma before a co-ordinating conjunction (or, and, but, for, yet, nor, etc.) in a compound sentence: I did my work, but I forgot to hand it in.

b. Use a comma between items (nouns, clauses, phrases, etc.) in a series of three or more, except before the last item when a conjunction is used: I bought apples, oranges, peaches, and bananas.

c. Use a comma between adjectives preceding a noun: This is a quiet, peaceful hotel. *Except,* if you cannot substitute *and* for the comma, do not use the comma: I have a small black cat.

d. Use a comma after an introductory modifier: Yes, I did it. Well, I'm going now.

e. Use a comma after an introductory prepositional phrase *only* if the phrase is long: In order to succeed in college and prepare for the future, one must study.

f. Use a comma to prevent misreading: Once inside, the dog began to bark.

g. Use commas to set off an appositive (an expression following a noun which means the same thing and can be used in place of the noun): Larry Jones, the student standing by the door, scored highest on the exam.

h. Use commas to set off a parenthetical statement (an expression inserted to explain or emphasize): Mary, for example, never studied. John, on the other hand, always did.

i. Use commas to set off a direct address: His comments, my dear friend, cannot be repeated.

j. Use commas to set off an expression inserted into a direct quotation: "Now," he said, "the class is dismissed."

k. Use a comma to show contrast: This is a college, not a university. She is a freshman, not a senior.

l. Use commas to set off a nonrestrictive clause or phrase (an expression which is not necessary for understanding, but does provide additional information): My mother, who is a teacher, came to see me.

m. Use commas to set off an absolute phrase (an expression consisting of a noun or pronoun and a participle which modifies the sentence as a whole): Weather permitting, we can study together tonight.

n. Use a comma before *such as* when it is used to introduce an example: She is interested in many occult subjects, such as magic, astrology, and mind reading.

3. The Semi-colon

a. Use a semi-colon to separate two independent clauses not joined by a conjunction: I went to see him; he was not there.

b. Use a semi-colon between equal elements that contain commas: John, president; Paula, vice-president; Jane, treasurer; etc.

4. The colon

Use a colon after a complete statement to draw attention to what follows: She had many hobbies: painting, swimming, tennis, and reading.

5. Quotation Marks

a. Use quotation marks before and after words which are exactly copied: "Well," Mary said, "this is a happy day." Note the position of the quotation marks *after* the comma and the period.

b. Use quotation marks to identify titles of essays, individual poems, songs, stories, etc., which are part of larger works.

6. The Hyphen

Use a hyphen between words used as a single modifier before a noun: He is a well-known writer. This is a half-finished job.

7. Underlining

Underline titles of books, magazines, and other complete works.

In addition to these basic rules, see the index for particular marks of punctuation discussed in various sections of this book.

FOOTNOTE & BIBLIOGRAPHY FORMS FOR SOCIAL & NATURAL SCIENCES

Most of the disciplines in the social and natural sciences such as anthropology, sociology, archeology, chemistry, etc., use a slightly different system of footnoting for the citation of sources and for the final bibliography. Some footnotes remain the same as on our sample paper: those that expand, cross-reference or define information do appear numbered at the bottom of the page or at the end of the section. However, simple citations for the purposes of identification are given in the text. Consult with your instructor or the journal for which you are writing to find out which system is preferred.

FORMS OF FOOTNOTES FOR CITATION OF SOURCES

Place of citation: Sources are given immediately following the material to be documented.

There is some evidence that primitive man expressed his inner reality in terms of outer symbols (Long 1963: 66-67), such as animals, sky or earth.

NOTE: Your reader can look in your bibliography under Long's publication of 1963 to find other facts of publication. It is clear that this material appeared on pages 66-67.

NOTE: If the authority's name is given in the text itself, only the date and page(s) are given in the parenthesis. If there is more than one work published in the same year by the same author, use a lower case letter after the date to distinguish them; for example (Campbell 1972 a).

Campbell (1972: 28-29) stresses western man's fear of looking within himself, whereas Long (1963) includes many myths of creation that show primitive man's interest in his inner state of consciousness.

FORMS FOR BIBLIOGRAPHICAL DATA

Papers in the social or natural sciences rarely use the term *Bibliography* for the list of works cited. Usually the term used is *List of References* or *Works Cited*, and only those works actually mentioned in the text are included.

Forms for "List of References"

1. Alphabetize by author.

2. List two or more works by the same author chronologically.

3. Put author's name on first line of entry followed by a colon.

4. Indent dates, followed by two spaces without punctuation, followed by title, publisher, place.

> NOTE: Use lower case letters for entries like those under Coe in the following illustration:

```
               List of References

Campbell, Joseph:
    1972    Myths to Live By, Viking Press, New York.
    1974    The Mythic Image, Princeton University
            Press, Princeton.

Coe, Michael D.:
    1957a   "Cycle 7 Monuments in Middle America: A Recon-
            sideration," American Anthropologist, vol.
            59, 4, pp. 597-611.
    1957b   "The Olmec Style," Handbook of Middle Ameri-
            can Studies, vol. 3, pp. 739-775, Univ. of
            Texas Press, Austin.
```

> NOTE: It is very simple to identify the work cited in the parenthetical documentation of the text.

In some disciplines the entries are numbered in the order that they are cited in the text; it is important to consult your instructor for variations.

INDEX

Introducing
Barron's Book Notes
The Smart Way to Study Literature

Everything you need for better understanding, better performance in class, better grades! Clear, concise, fun to read — Barron's Book Notes make literature come alive.

100 titles to choose from:

THE AENEID
ALL QUIET ON THE WESTERN FRONT
ALL THE KING'S MEN
ANIMAL FARM
ANNA KARENINA
AS I LAY DYING
AS YOU LIKE IT
BABBITT
BEOWULF
BILLY BUDD & TYPEE
BRAVE NEW WORLD
CANDIDE
CANTERBURY TALES
CATCH-22
THE CATCHER IN THE RYE
CRIME AND PUNISHMENT
THE CRUCIBLE
CRY, THE BELOVED COUNTRY
DAISY MILLER & TURN OF THE SCREW
DAVID COPPERFIELD
DEATH OF A SALESMAN
THE DIVINE COMEDY: THE INFERNO
DOCTOR FAUSTUS
A DOLL'S HOUSE & HEDDA GABLER
DON QUIXOTE
ETHAN FROME
A FAREWELL TO ARMS
FAUST: PARTS I AND II
FOR WHOM THE BELL TOLLS
THE GLASS MENAGERIE & A STREETCAR NAMED DESIRE
THE GOOD EARTH
THE GRAPES OF WRATH
GREAT EXPECTATIONS

THE GREAT GATSBY
GULLIVER'S TRAVELS
HAMLET
HARD TIMES
HEART OF DARKNESS & THE SECRET SHARER
HENRY IV, PART 1
THE HOUSE OF THE SEVEN GABLES
HUCKLEBERRY FINN
THE ILIAD
INVISIBLE MAN
JANE EYRE
JULIUS CAESAR
THE JUNGLE
KING LEAR
LIGHT IN AUGUST
LORD JIM
LORD OF THE FLIES
THE LORD OF THE RINGS & THE HOBBIT
MACBETH
MADAME BOVARY
THE MAYOR OF CASTERBRIDGE
THE MERCHANT OF VENICE
A MIDSUMMER NIGHT'S DREAM
MOBY DICK
MY ANTONIA
NATIVE SON
NEW TESTAMENT
1984
THE ODYSSEY
OEDIPUS TRILOGY
OF MICE AND MEN
THE OLD MAN AND THE SEA
OLD TESTAMENT
OLIVER TWIST

ONE FLEW OVER THE CUCKOO'S NEST
OTHELLO
OUR TOWN
PARADISE LOST
THE PEARL
PORTRAIT OF THE ARTIST AS A YOUNG MAN
PRIDE AND PREJUDICE
THE PRINCE
THE RED BADGE OF COURAGE
THE REPUBLIC
RETURN OF THE NATIVE
RICHARD III
ROMEO AND JULIET
THE SCARLET LETTER
A SEPARATE PEACE
SILAS MARNER
SLAUGHTERHOUSE FIVE
SONS AND LOVERS
THE SOUND AND THE FURY
STEPPENWOLF & SIDDHARTHA
THE STRANGER
THE SUN ALSO RISES
A TALE OF TWO CITIES
THE TAMING OF THE SHREW
THE TEMPEST
TESS OF THE D'URBERVILLES
TO KILL A MOCKINGBIRD
TOM JONES
TOM SAWYER
TWELFTH NIGHT
WALDEN
WHO'S AFRAID OF VIRGINIA WOOLF?
WUTHERING HEIGHTS

Only $2.50 each!
On sale at your local bookstore.

BARRON'S
113 Crossways Park Drive
Woodbury, NY 11797

ENGLISH LANGUAGE GUIDES from  BARRON'S

☐ **A POCKET GUIDE TO CORRECT ENGLISH**
Michael Temple
Rules for correct grammar and usage, spelling, writing, and other essentials of English. Contrasting right and wrong examples help you avoid common mistakes. (2425-7) $2.95

☐ **A POCKET GUIDE TO CORRECT GRAMMAR**
Vincent Hopper
Parts of speech, punctuation, correct usage, and common mistakes are analyzed and clarified in this handy reference guide. (2849-X) $2.95

☐ **A POCKET GUIDE TO CORRECT PUNCTUATION**
Robert Brittain
This long-needed guide explains what each punctuation mark means and how it is used. The many examples help drive home key points. (2599-7) $2.95

☐ **A POCKET GUIDE TO CORRECT SPELLING**
Francis Griffith
Valuable reference tool with a listing of 25,000 commonly misspelled words, plus a helpful section on spelling rules, capitalization, abbreviation, and more. (2620-9) $2.95

☐ **A POCKET GUIDE TO VOCABULARY**
Brownstein and Weiner
3,000 words that every educated person should know — the same words that appear on standardized exams like the SAT. (2814-7) $2.95

10 Steps in Writing the Research Paper
Markman and Waddell   160 pp., $4.50
The process of writing a research paper is reduced to 10 simple steps. Plus a unique section on "Plagiarism: A Step to Avoid."

The Art of Styling Sentences: 20 Patterns to Success
Wadell, Esch, and Walker
112 pp., $4.95
By imitating 20 sentence patterns and variations, students will grasp how to write with imagination, clarity, and style. Illustrated with practice material for writing more effectively.

Spelling Your Way to Success
Mersand and Griffith   224 pp., $5.95
A systematic, simplified, and progressive method of improving one's spelling without constantly having to consult a dictionary. Numerous self-tests and practice material.

Building an Effective Vocabulary
Cedric Gale   288 pp., $4.95
A thorough course in all the methods of evaluating words for richness and appropriateness to improve ability to communicate.

1001 Pitfalls in English Grammar
Vincent F. Hopper   352 pp., $5.95
The most common errors in the English language are examined, including grammar, spelling, word choice, and punctuation.

1100 Words You Need to Know
Bromberg and Gordon   220 pp., $5.95
More than 1100 words and idioms taken from the mass media and introduced in readable stories. Contains 46 daily lessons of 20 minutes each.

Essentials of English
Hopper, Foote, Gale   256 pp., $4.95
A comprehensive program in the writing skills necessary for effective communication.

Essentials of Writing
Hopper and Gale   176 pp., $5.95
A companion workbook for the material in ESSENTIALS OF ENGLISH.

Word Mastery: A Guide to the Understanding of Words
Drabkin, Bromberg   224 pp., $6.95
This fascinating book stresses word use and word development through the presentation of words in natural settings such as newspapers and magazines. With practice exercises.

How to Write Themes and Term Papers
Barbara Lenmark Ellis 160 pp., $4.95
The correct, logical approach to tackling a theme project or paper.

Words with a Flair
Bromberg and Liebb   224 pp., $6.95
A collection of 600 difficult but useful words. Includes word games and puzzles.

STUDY GUIDES from BARRON'S

☐ **HOW TO SUCCEED IN HIGH SCHOOL: A Practical Guide to Better Grades**
George Weigand
This comprehensive self-help guide teaches effective study techniques for English, foreign languages, math, science, and history; gives information on planning study time, making good notes, and taking tests successfully; offers advice on preparing for college and careers.   (0078-1) $3.50

☐ **STRATEGIES FOR TAKING TESTS**
James H. Divine and Judy Divine
384 pp.
Designed to boost test scores, this new test prep guide approaches test taking, not through guesswork and gamesmanship, but by helping students get acquainted with the fixed number of question types used on standardized exams.   (2565-2) $8.95

☐ **STUDY TACTICS**
William H. Armstrong and M. W. Lampe
For students who want to earn higher grades, this useful guide presents an easy-to-follow plan for sound study habits. Pointers on mastering writing techniques, increasing reading speed, reviewing for exams, and more.
          (2590-3) $4.95

☐ **STUDENT SUCCESS SECRETS**
Eric Jensen
This dynamic book uses the techniques of self-hypnosis to help students build motivation, self-confidence, and the basic skills essential to academic success. Written by the founder/president of a leading educational firm, the book offers valuable advice on test taking, studying, reading, writing, and note taking, as well as the personal habits that lead to success in school and in life.
          (2589-X) $4.95

Buy them at your local bookstore or
use coupon on next page for ordering.

☐ **YOU CAN SUCCEED! The Ultimate Study Guide for Students**
Eric Jensen
This positive guide to success in school encourages high school students to make a contract with themselves to set goals and work ambitiously toward them. Among the topics covered: Lack of Motivation--the #1 Problem, Success Habits, Attack Plan for Studying, Using Your Memory More Effectively, Word Power, How to Take Tests.　　　　　　　　　(2084-7) $3.95

☐ **STUDY TIPS: How to Study Effectively and Get Better Grades**
Armstrong and Lampe
A guide to improving the skills necessary to earn higher grades in many subjects at many levels. Tips on how to master writing techniques, improve study habits, increase reading speed, review for exams, and more　　(2366-5) $3.95